Invisible Truth

Tapping into
The Supreme Source of
Infinite Manifestation

Christina Wollebek-Smith
with Marty Smith

MIKE —
THANK YOU. YOUR HELP AS
OUR 'GO TO' WAS MORE THAN
APPRECIATED.
MARTY

Revised 2017. Book jacket design by Nicole Miller.

10 9 8 7 6 5 4 3 2 1

Library of Congress Cataloging-in-Publication Data: 2011905421

ISBN-13: 978-1461048688
ISBN-10: 1461048680

Dedicated to the visionary and rebel in our souls.

Contents

Part Four: Even More Stuff

Acknowledgments

First, I would like to thank Michael. This man came into my life in a most unexpected way. For me, it was he who first started espousing the laws and principles of the universe being in alignment with the principles of faith. The more we talked, the more intrigued I became. His passion and intensity were exhilarating. With Michael I learned about applying the true meaning of Invisible Truth in lucid, clear and easy to understand terms.

After recording the Invisible Truth CD set, it became increasingly apparent that this systematic approach must be written in a book form to fully explain the concepts of this applicable philosophy. I turned to my longtime friend, the father of my children, Marty Smith. Over all of the years I have known him, Marty has studied the bible voraciously, has been a successful publisher, and has written many stories. I knew Marty was the one to write this book.

In addition, I would like to express my gratitude to our editor Theresa Wyne for her unflagging patience in the process, as well as her father, Michael Wyne, for his technical assistance in writing this book.

My children, Rachael and Sean. These two have taught me more about what miracles are than anyone else has. They taught me the true meaning of thankfulness. They are my joy and essence of love today and forever.

Invisible Truth
Prologue

- The world of science and the world of religion (faith) are not exclusive. They're congruent. They're symbiotic.

- Science has proof positive that all of the universe is made up of energy, including the human race. The various faiths of the world concur.

- Energy cannot be created nor can it be destroyed. Its direction, however, can be changed.

- The Nine Laws and Principles of Invisible Truth explain how to redirect energy in a way that creates (manifests) controlled results through understanding our power.

- The essential message is to change our conscious redirection of energy. Invisible Truth is a study of creating change within ourselves, and therefore the universe.

Part One

In the Beginning

What Is the Invisible Truth?

How's it working for you so far? Your life, that is?

We have worked hard our entire lives to become precisely who we are. We have arrived. Have we attained peace?

We live in our version of the universe's truth. How does it feel? Does it bring us harmony?

Whose truth is it? Our truth? My truth? The Invisible Truth is the real truth. The truth that is not rationalized, plagiarized or justified. The truth that is energy in its purest form.

The Invisible Truth is revealed to us when we redirect our energy to construct the reality of the true, inner peace we desire.

Stop chasing peace. It is ours. We won. We are here.

Peace results from us reorganizing all of our energy into the constraints of our own choosing.

What is the Invisible Truth?

Peace.

It is peace at the core of my being. Harmony in my soul. That's the truth.

And that is true freedom.

Argue for your limitations, and sure enough, they're yours.
— Richard Bach

The Possibilities

What if there is another way?

What if the reality we have created can be changed into what we desire it to be? What if we can actually live out our dreams and forge peace in doing so?

We can.

Reality is what we have created from what we have experienced. It is our truth. To begin the process of changing our reality into the future we desire is so very simple. As Nike says, just do it. Invisible Truth shows us how.

It is time for us to stop defending all that we believe to be true. It is time to release all that does not work in our lives.

The real truth is either yes or no, off or on, is or is not. The universal truth, God's truth, is either black or white. Yet, we live our lives in the gray area between the universe's truth and our guilty version. Between what is real and what is our chaos.

It is calming when we realize that the real truth and our invented truth are not necessarily the same. We own our truth…it is ours.

However, while we realize that our truth is that which we have created, there is a real truth that will not be denied.

That is the truth of the universe, of God, of nature. It is the basis of the laws of nature, of science, of reality. Accepting that our truth and the real truth are not in alignment, we are free to seek the real truth in any manner we wish. We are now free of the experiences, rationalizations and justifications of "our truth."

With freedom comes peace.

We are no longer bound by the justified constrictions of "our" reality. We are no longer tied to the random rules of "my" reality. We are now free to explore all of the possibilities and potentials of the universe. In so doing, we are exploring the Invisible Truth.

As soon as we realize that our truth isn't necessarily "the truth," we lower our defenses. By relaxing our defensive posture, we instantly allow for all of the universe, and our life within it, to focus. We begin our journey toward the real truth.

All we have to do to begin the adventure toward the real truth is to change our minds. That starts by asking a simple question.

How's it working for you so far? Your life, that is?

Examine our lives. Evaluate our truth. Focus.

It is time to take down our pretenses and stop rationalizing; there's no one here to impress but ourselves. Decide which parts of our life we are going to change now. No holding back. It is time for an honest change or we would not be holding this book in our hands.

In front of us is only directed, organized energy. We are refocusing and we are changing from this point forward.

We are free.

With each day we come one day closer to finding out what is really "on the other side." Some of us have actually considered finding out in an unnatural hurry; some of us don't know if we wish to play here anymore. Relax, my friend. It is just a game. Don't take life so seriously.

> *"No reason to get excited,"*
> *The thief, he kindly spoke,*
> *"There are many here among us*
> *Who feel that life is but a joke*
> *But you and I, we've been through that*

And this is not our fate
So let us stop talking falsely now, the hour is getting late."
— Along the Watchtower. Performed by
Bob Dylan and by Jimi Hendrix.
Written by Bob Dylan.

Life is not a joke...but we have been through that chaos. It is, however, nothing more than a lifelong game. It is nothing more than a momentary blip on the radar screen of all of creation. In the big scheme of things, in the history of the universe, in the history of all creation, what does our existence mean?

The answer is different than we may think. Our existence is extremely significant to the outcome of the universe.

We do matter.

Having said that, our time on this earth in this current vessel holding our being is nothing more than a grain of sand in the Sahara Desert of time and space. The hour is getting late so let's stop talking falsely. We have spent enough of our lives' minutes doing that. It is time for us to get ahold of the big picture, and change the universe for the better.

That is the hope of mankind. That is the singular hope for us.

The Nine Laws and Principles of Invisible Truth

The Invisible Truth Alliance began in 2006 as a way for a think tank to apply the nine laws and principles in a systematic way.

When the recordings of Invisible Truth came out and focus groups gathered around it to comment on its content the comment that came out most often was...silence.

The simplicity of what had been put together was stunning in its approach, and visionary in its message. From the concept of these recordings came the production of this book.

The course is complete. Thousands of the recorded versions have been distributed. It is revolutionizing the way people create their lives.

Much of the reading in this book is easy and obvious. Some of the reading is heavy. It is necessary to instill logic and philosophy in order to make our stance clear. We felt it necessary to spell out the entire position of Invisible Truth to give an in-depth reasoning behind the statements we are making.

Not only do we spell out the premise behind Invisible Truth, we give people the step-by-step tools to begin their own exploration to find the questions they are looking for. As we will see in this text, we do not profess to know what all the answers are. What we do is give guidelines to clarifying the real questions…in our desire to know the real truth.

Invisible Truth allows us to step out of the herd. It clears the confusion running rampant through our minds. It allows us to see where we are now, discover who we are and decide what we are. We then propel the adventure of getting to where we desire to be.

The Adventure

We are here. We have chosen to come on a journey. We have made the right choice. We are going to go find the magic that has eluded us for so long. By stepping forward, we have decided to find the Invisible Truth.

We have chosen freedom.

We have chosen freedom from our past. We have chosen freedom from our future. We have chosen to be here, right now…right this second.

We have chosen to understand and control the way we think, the way we speak, and the way we believe. We have chosen to work toward that which we desire to manifest in our lives while understanding that manifesting all we desire starts with forgiveness.

We have chosen to be thankful for all we have, and all that we receive, while understanding that the only way to receive is to give.

We have also chosen to understand and control our environment. We have chosen freedom to create all that we ever desired...in abundance.

We have chosen greatness.

Believe it or not, we have just gone through a review of all of the nine laws and principles of Invisible Truth. The truth is as easy as that. All we have to do is choose to start.

The journey begins with understanding that this is for the rest of our lives. This is not a "fix it" kind of study. This is a lifestyle. It is not for five minutes of affirmations each morning; it is for every minute of every hour of every day.

This is not a religion; it is an applied philosophy. This study does not give us the answer; it helps with the question.

We can live by these laws and principles outlined in Invisible Truth, or we can play with them. None of the laws and principles are anything that people are unfamiliar with. All we do in this text is explain them in a way that makes sense.

This is a way of life. To reach our highest level of awareness, this system must be absorbed into our very core at a cellular level.

Read these laws and principles and integrate them. This is the key. The rest of this book gives our stance, and the reasoning behind our stance. It is good reading and it will help us understand how to change our lives...forever.

The Truth

The truth, as it was. We are addicts. We are addicted to the way we think, act and react. We are programmed, autopilot machines taught, through experience, to automatically process all that comes to us.

The confusion in our minds takes the form of random, compulsive, disorganized energy. That pandemonium enslaves us to reactions that keep us from our desires. The energy with which we create our universe becomes trapped in a reactive cycle of negative flow that attracts vibrations of a similar magnitude towards us.

There is some confusion between our previous truths and real truth. That is where the Invisible Truth lies.

John 14:16-18 And I will ask the Father, and he will give you another Counselor to be with you forever — the Spirit of truth. The world cannot accept him, because it neither sees him nor knows him. But you know him, for he lives with you and will be in you. I will not leave you as orphans; I will come to you. (NIV)

John 8:32 Then you will know the truth, and the truth will set you free." (NIV)

I choose greatness.
I choose enthusiasm, inspiration and joy.
I choose health, wealth and happiness.
I choose freedom.

"Our deepest fear is not that we are inadequate. Our deepest fear is that we are powerful beyond measure. It is our light, not our darkness that most frightens us. We ask ourselves, Who am I to be brilliant, gorgeous, talented, fabulous?
Actually, who are you not to be? You are a child of God. Your playing small does not serve the world. There is nothing enlightened about shrinking so that other people won't feel insecure around you. We are all meant to shine, as children do. We

were born to make manifest the glory of God that is within us. It is not just in some of us; it is in everyone."
— Marianne Williamson

The nine laws and principles are a symbiotic approach. Though each is a complete thought in and of itself, it is important that when we start our study of these laws and principles, we start with *The Bucket* and move to *Living in the Now*.

It is essential that we integrate all nine laws and principles into our lives. Think of each as a different section of the orchestra. Each section has its own harmony in itself, but when the harmonies of each section are brought together as a whole, we create the magic of the music envisioned by the ultimate composer.

In the Beginning

It is time to harness the power of God, the scientific universe and ourselves.

Energy

There are over seven billion of us running around this planet. Seven billion "bundles of conscious energy" who process thought, enact words and have beliefs. Seven billion sets of beliefs. Not a single one of them identical to another.

This is the one constant in the universe. Energy. Energy cannot be created nor destroyed. It can, however, change directions. It is easier and more productive to redirect energy than to resist it. We are going to learn to direct the change in energy, in our lives and in the world.

It is our energy. We can redirect it to control the flow of our lives. Permanently.

From the very moment of creation, within the womb we are gathering information upon which to base our decisions on how to act within any given set of circumstances. From the time we are born, through our early years, we form much of the basis for our beliefs.

Our beliefs create our energy. Our energy creates our world. The energy of the populace of the world creates the environment we live in. We, as a society, as a world, have let the power (energy) of others create the parameters within which we live. It is time to think outside the box. It is time to take back our power.

Taking our power back starts within.

The flow and impact of energy is a principle of physics. Einstein I'm not, but I do understand that the direction, mass and velocity (momentum) of energy is changed every second, in all things. One of the few things I remember from science class is that for every action (energy), there is an equal and opposite reaction.

The Basic Premise

The basic premise of Invisible Truth is that we can be the agent of that change (redirection), in the direction we choose (action), and not be a victim of fate (reaction). Further, we are now learning to use the direction of energy in concert with its flow, manipulating it to our advantage instead of resisting it to our detriment.

For example, the martial art of Aikido is about flowing with the momentum of the energy coming at us, taking control of that energy, and then redirecting it into a motion that we desire.

This we will do with the energy in all parts of our lives. Redirect it.

Living in the Herd

Society requires a "herd" mentality. In order to live in the herd, humanity has created a standard by which we are taught to behave. The system taught to us sets the parameters of our belief system through which we judge ourselves and the world around us.

Though the requirements of living within the "herd" are set for a reason, and rightfully so, the realization that we are being herded is somewhat disturbing.

Invisible Truth sets out to define our common reality as it relates to our conscious mind and how our subconscious mind affects our own lives and our world.

We will learn to go with the momentum, the flow, then turn it to our advantage.

Invisible Truth defines for us the reality of the energy we live in, and the means of redirecting the energy by controlling and directing it in the way we desire, thereby creating the result we choose.

How Did We Get Here?

When we are very young and have no experience through which to judge our world, we are sponges. We do nothing but absorb. Think about having seen a small child stop what they are doing, stand perfectly still and just watch something. There is no judgment. They are just absorbing whatever it is that they are observing for the first time.

That small child, at that very moment, is forming a belief. They are seeing an action, a reaction and its consequence. Around the consequence, that child wraps an emotion. Through the emotion they are feeling, whether it is joy, sorrow, happiness or hurt, they create a judgment. They begin to categorize similar experiences through that which they have already observed. They are creating a filter through which they view the world. They are creating a neural pathway.

Think for a minute. Go back to our own childhoods. Find that specific moment of utter and utmost bliss. Feel the world around us. Smell the same smells. Hear the sounds. Hold onto that moment for just a minute. Feel the emotions. Smell the air around us. Feel the temperature on our faces. Feel the moment in time so long ago. Cherish it.

Now, think of another moment, one that we don't like to recall, the one we cringe away from. The screaming, fighting and anger. Think about how that made us feel…just for a second. Now, let it go.

We carry these moments with us, be they burdens or beautifications. They affect our perception, from before our earliest recollections.

We got to where we are now through the system of our consciousness. As energy comes to us, we generate a filter through which all of the consequences of that energy flow. The filter is called our subconscious.

Through the patterns of our thought (energy) process, we become "addicted" to how we process the information we absorb. That process, that "addiction," that filtering system, creates a jumble of thoughts and emotions that are random, compulsive and disorganized.

We will learn to change the random, compulsive, disorganized energy in our lives into directed, controlled, organized energy to manifest the results we desire. We learn to "lasso" the direction of energy as it flows through us, manipulating the directional change of that energy through conscious awareness and discipline. We learn to control the consequence, and thereby the "cause," within our lives.

Our Energy Starts in the Womb

I so fondly remember watching my children in their very young years. When I saw them stop and watch, I would become aware of what they were watching, and just observe them in awe. Often it was a moment of others playing they would absorb, with a look of sheer wonderment in their eyes. It would always move me, sometimes to tears.

I remember one time I brought my daughter with me when I went out to visit a construction site when I was a partner in a masonry company which specialized in restoration.

It was a residential site and the masons were working on the front of the house near the front door. It was a safe environment, so I set my daughter (18 months old) down and let her play on the lawn.

The masons were busy so they greeted me and kept on with what they were doing. I was talking to the lead man as the masons worked, and I noticed his eyes were not on mine. He was looking at my daughter and smiling. When I turned to look at her also, I saw that she was standing perfectly still, watching the men tuck pointing (hand tooling mortar into brick joints). We laughed and continued our conversation.

As the masons finished their work, they stopped and walked to where we were to chat and greet my daughter (who had all the men in the company wrapped around her little finger). We were talking about the job when the lead started laughing again.

We turned to see Rachael had walked to the wall, reached into a bucket of mortar, grabbed a tool, and with great pleasure, was taking mortar out of the bucket and putting it onto the wall…and doing a pretty good job of it. The only reason she missed some of the mortar joints was because she was jumping up and down with glee. We all laughed as I warned the masons that they were all replaceable. That only set Rachael's reputation in stone, so to speak.

Rachael observed something new, did it herself, had fun doing it, and was rewarded with the positive reinforcement of the people around her. No, she didn't become a mason, but she has a positive experience through which she enjoys seeing brick work being done. Now that she has grown, when she sees one of the masons from the old days, they "talk shop" and her happiness glows.

Remember, she was only 18 months old. Association begins in the womb.

Before we even start school, we are absorbing how our parent(s) view the world and react to the events of their lives. We learn fear, anger, joy, happiness and everything in between. More importantly, we learn the triggers of these emotions, and begin to set our belief systems.

When we start school, we are being taught the thoughts, therefore the beliefs, of others as we continue the learning process of our lives. Our judgments begin to lock in the way we see things. It is either black or it is white. It is bad or it is good. It is happy or it is sad.

Two people looking at the same thing might experience two different sets of emotions. One may see it as a good thing and have positive energy around an occurrence, while another may see the same thing as truly detrimental. Regardless of what the event is, the emotion and all that is wrapped around that emotion is, seemingly, set in stone.

Whatever "it" is, we have a pathway through which to process the information being fed to us. These set (neural) pathways are the way by which we judge the information (energy) being absorbed. Some of the pathways create a "block" for which information, or stimuli, which could be useful to us is shut out because we have a preconceived notion (erroneous pathway) of what that specific stimulus means to us.

We created our pathways (beliefs) to assist us. Some do. The struggles we have in our lives are based around the pathways we have created that don't work, are inaccurate, or are no longer valid.

Some we inherited or were taught as children. That doesn't mean we have to keep them. When we broke our toys and were told that "money doesn't grow on trees," we kept that pathway from which we now hear ourselves say that "abundance is limited."

Abundance of any kind is unlimited. God said so. It is how we choose to view our ability to create that is limited.

Where Science and Religion Fit in

Science forms the basis of beliefs for many. Religion forms the basis of beliefs for others. Life experience, for all of us, forms yet another set of beliefs. Some require hard scientific proof and have no room for mystic speculation. Other "bundles of conscious energy" base their entire life equation on faith. Most of us vacillate somewhere in between.

Science is based on the principle of cause and effect. Yes, there are theories and hypotheses on which the scientists base their conjectures. However, until those theories and hypotheses are proven with empirical facts, it can be argued that these conjectures are nothing more than speculations or educated guesses.

Empirical facts are those that are provable or verifiable through experience or experiment. Proof, for the scientific mind, means being absolutely certain that "if this happens, then that will happen." The scientific mind desires to know the outcome of any given action in order to recreate an action that will give them a predictable result.

Empirical facts: that which are provable or verifiable through experience or experiment.

Particular religions base their faith on what they see as the infallible word of the teachings to which they adhere. Oddly, the faith based mind is not that different than that of a science based mind. The difference is a faith based mind is usually far more optimistic.

"If I believe this, then that will be the result."

Faith does not require proof…or does it? Do we? The faith based mind observes the world through a system of beliefs that shows the result they desire. True belief is knowing what the result of a specific action is going to be.

The scientific mind *desires to know* what the results of a specific action are. The faith based mind *knows* what the results of a specific action are.

Religion versus science. The age old dilemma.

In Invisible Truth, we set out to show that these two ideas, faith and science, are not necessarily exclusive nor contradictory. In fact, we will show that they, by their nature, are utterly interdependent. They are symbiotic.

The Science of Religion

It is a given that everything in the universe that we know of, or understand at a practical level, is made up of energy. The page we are reading is energy. The spicy chicken we smell grilling is energy. The laugh we had with an old friend is energy. The great sex with our spouses last night is energy. The smile we just had reading this is energy. We are energy. Our energy is great enough to give off heat radiating at around 98.6 degrees for, during a normal life span, somewhere between 50 to 100 years. That is an exorbitant amount of energy.

Energy is everywhere. The universe, both science and religion agree, is made up of energy. The space or air between our eyes and the page we are looking at right now is energy. The space of energy around us, the space that holds the world's energy, is called Aether. (ey-ther: "ey" is pronounced as a long A, as in fate.) Aether has been described as a fine gas made up of the smallest particles, or units, of matter.

DNA. Atoms. Molecules. Electrons. We know they are there. We can't see them. They have been scientifically proven to exist. The majority of the world takes it on faith that what the science books have taught us to believe is true, even though we can't see it.

Let's close our eyes. Feel the aether? Suck in a large breath of it. Let's hold our breaths. Feel the aether, the oxygen, the particles, fill our lungs. Feel the pulsation of cells, of molecules? Feel the desire to move the aether? That is energy. Energy is not stagnant. Though we can't see it, we "take it on faith" that we use that energy.

Fascinatingly, another definition of aether is the rarified element that filled both the heavens and the upper atmospheres of space.

A Definition of Energy

One of the definitions states that energy is the potential forces, inherent power and those forces' capacity for doing work and their ability to cause change.

There are many different forms of energy. There is light energy, mechanical energy, electrical energy, etc. However, it is all based on the same principles that govern all matter in the universe.

On Earth, all matter is based on a carbon form. All carbon forms interact with each other in what we call energy. Scientists can split fine hairs as to how this all interacts, but the fact is, this planet has a hyperactive, carbon interaction creating (redirecting) a great deal of energy.

We are bundles of conscious energy. Even in death, decomposition creates energy. In fact, without death and decay, energy as we know it would not be possible. The car we drive is powered by the decomposition of living organisms from another time. Energy. It is everywhere. Energy cannot be created or destroyed. However, energy does move from one form to another. It can change direction. We are the cause of the change of direction of energy in our lives. The direction of the change is within our control.

We are energy. This is a given. Another given is that energy is in constant motion and vibration. There are an incalculable number of levels of vibration. Without getting into the entire explanation of vibration, simply said, "like kind vibrations," or vibrations of the same, or similar, magnitude will attract. Dissimilar vibration, or vibration of a different magnitude, will repel.

Like attracts like…in the world of science as well.

Think of magnets that we played with as kids. If we put them together one way they came together hard, but if we attempted to put them together the opposite way, they were repelled. We are sure that there ought to be exceptions to this in the scientific world, but as a general correlation, this statement is true. Like attracts like.

There is no mystery to the universe. All things are made up of energy. The direction and form of energy is changed through cause and effect. This statement is empirically true, and is the basis on which science is founded. Science is the study of cause and effect.

We will learn to be the cause instead of the effect.

Religion

Most major religions of the world profess that God is omnipresent (everywhere), omniscient (all knowledgeable), and omnipotent (all powerful). Therefore, God is both unlimited and abundant (an over-sufficient supply). Given this statement, logic dictates that if God is abundant, and God is unlimited, then God's abundance is unlimited.

God is also omnificent. He has and is creating all things; He has unlimited powers of creation. Within our lives, so do we.

Those who believe in God (and those who don't) create fear, anger and stress in their lives and the lives of those around them, and the energy field they live in while attempting to compete with others for an abundance that they believe is limited. That *they* believe is limited.

However, if they lived by their faith…that deserves repetition. However. If they lived by their faith…big *if*. If they lived by their faith, they would know that there is no limited abundance.

To limit abundance is to limit God. To limit God is to limit the omnipotent power of God. In limiting the omnipotent power of God, a person of faith is going against the direct nature of what they believe.

This is the ultimate contradiction of mankind.

To diminish the omnipotence of God is to question our faith.

Abundance

We can have abundance in anything. It can be abundant health. It can be abundant happiness. It can be anything we choose to have in abundance. Abundance is unlimited (God says so). It is our choice. We are given the choice to manifest abundance.

The Teachings of the Bible

Deuteronomy 8:18 But remember the Lord your God, for it is he who gives you the ability to produce wealth, and so confirms his covenant, which he swore to your forefathers, as it is today. (NIV)

Let's start right out with the question on many people's minds these days. Cut straight to the chase. God gave us the power to create wealth. Each has their own definition of wealth. Good. Whatever that definition, He has given us the power to create it.

To doubt that is to doubt our own faith. He did not limit our power. He gave us the power, all that we require. Yet, we diminish the power by not following the principles set forth before us. Having faith alone will not do it. Wishing for wealth, alone, will not do it. Faith is action. Action is energy. Invisible Truth shows us how to move directed, organized energy to change our lives to what we would like them to be.

Directed, organized energy. Think on that for a moment. It is self-evident. Faith is action. Action is energy. True faith is directed, organized energy.

Psalms 78:41 Again and again they put God to the test; they vexed the Holy One of Israel. (NIV)

We are the ones who limit God in our lives. He has allowed us unlimited abundance. Both scientifically and scripturally, this book shows us how to use choice and the principles, laws and applications of nature, to create God's unlimited power of manifestation of abundance. "The applications of nature" is the recognition of the energy around everything in our world and how we affect its direction.

Read this paragraph again. Grasp it. Own it.

Once we own this statement, we learn to increase our income, create powerful and wonderful relationships, and increase harmony and peace within ourselves and in our lives.

We learn effective, long-term technologies to tap into the unlimited abundance that we desire, no matter what our situation looks like at any given time. We WILL be able to tap into our abundance, consciously, willfully and wittingly. In charge. Directed, organized energy.

We are in charge. Emphatically...the cause of energy, not the effect.

Using Invisible Truth

Read each section of Invisible Truth in its entirety. To create a habit one must repeat the lessons many times. Particular laws and principles that have been read or heard elsewhere are reinforced through repeated reference and reorganization in order to ingrain them into our thinking. It is then that these laws and principles become crystal clear and part of our makeup as a person.

The integration of these laws and principles is a method by which we take control of our lives. It is a new fresh way to think of the connection between the laws of the universe and the laws and principles of our faith.

The cause and effect of the Laws of Faith are, indeed, the same as the Laws of the Universe and the Laws of Science.

The further we go into this course of enlightenment, the clearer the understanding becomes. At some point it will hit us and we will know when that happens. We will smile, possibly laugh out loud, and look up from the text with a definite AH-HA moment. The world will look different. The focus will be different.

Because of the amount of information given, we recommend that everyone reads this course over and over again. Remember, we are creating new habits. These new habits are created through new, associative, neural pathways. Though we might think we understand a concept after reading it once, it is very possible that, though we have had some miraculous AH-HA moments, we have yet to fully grasp the concept until we have been through it two, three or four times, maybe more. Continue moving forward and we will see steady progress toward our desired vision.

Keep asking ourselves about the patterns we have created in our lives to date, as we do all the time. "How is it working for me so far?"

That "yard stick" by which we measure our failures, by which we compare ourselves to our neighbors, by which we always find ourselves lacking, is gone.

Creating positive energy in our lives is a lifelong process. These laws and principles are not an immediate "fix." This is a way to "let God out" from our inner being and allow us to choose to do His work...for the rest of our lives.

We have found that these teachings are so concentrated and powerful that while we are taking notes and thinking about something that we have just read, there is a good chance that we will miss something important. In many of the test panels people have stated that since there is so much good information and so many good references within this text they have had a hard time grasping them all in a continuous read.

Read the lessons all the way through the first time. Then, go back and read each chapter individually. If necessary, read it again. Absorb it into the core of our being. Contemplate how it relates to our lives. Think about how changing each specific pattern in our lives will move us further toward where we choose to be.

Keep reading. Absorb these laws and principles. Watch as they become life altering methods by which our worlds change for the better.

Manifestation

To start this journey, we are required to understand certain words. I would like to introduce the concept of manifestation.

Manifestation: an act of manifesting; the state of being manifested; an outward and perceptible indication; a materialization.

Manifest: to make clear or evident to the eye or the understanding; show plainly; to show or demonstrate plainly; reveal.

Materialization: the process of coming into being; the appearance of a bodily form; something that comes into existence as a result.

Karma: Hinduism, Buddhism. Action, seen as bringing upon oneself an inevitable result, good or bad, either in this life or in a reincarnation. In Theosophy: the cosmic principle according to which each person is rewarded or punished in one incarnation according to that person's deeds in the previous incarnation. In Eastern religions and Western philosophies: thought of as fate or destiny. The good or bad emanations felt to be generated by someone or something.

It is so intense that it is considered to emanate from us. In some of the Eastern religions, our Karma is thought to be so strong that it is almost visible to a discerning eye, as in the phrase "to see our aura."

Our Karma: What is it? Put a word to it. What does it look like? Be specific. Write it down. It will change...soon.

We use the word manifesting because it more closely symbolizes the spiritual and physical properties of these laws than the word materialization. Materialization indicates that an object appears for no reason. Manifestation indicates that an object appears with intent.

Our intent, our intention, our manifestation.

The concept of manifestation starts with understanding that there are certain laws and principles set in the universe. These laws and principles are all based around energy and the dynamics of how energy works. When we learn to harness these laws and principles we will reap what we choose at an accelerated rate .

Understand this first. Our subconscious mind is made up of the materials fed to us by our conscious mind. Our subconscious mind is the thing that gives our reaction, which in turn creates the actions of our conscious mind.

Our survival, and that of our ancestors, has been fully predicated on the reactions of our subconscious mind. The "fight or flight" instincts of our ancestors allowed them to survive all the dangers that surrounded them. Those same instincts allowed them to hunt the beasts they feared in order to provide meat.

When I smell cookies baking anywhere in the world (conscious mind), I travel straight back to my mother's kitchen (subconscious mind), where I felt warm and loved. I then investigate where the smell is coming from and find a way to swipe a cookie…kidding. That was the eight year old in me talking. Mom would catch me and I would run like a rabbit and she would laugh and attempt to swat me with the wooden spoon.

What really happens is that when I smell those cookies, no matter what my mindset is at the moment, I am overwhelmed with a feeling of being protected and loved.

Invisible Truth is not about making all subconscious conscious; it is about consciously massaging the subconscious to form a base on which to manifest karmic results in the exact way we desire.

Put another way, Invisible Truth teaches us to materialize the results we desire by mentally controlling the directed, organized energy process that creates the results in our lives. We are learning to create patterns of energy that allow our universe to open in a way never before available to us. We begin to achieve our goals.

There is a difference between surviving and thriving. Our genetic disposition has allowed us to survive the Law of the Jungle (Darwin's survival of the fittest), throughout the generations, since the beginning of time. Because we are here, we have earned the right to thrive. Being a victim is not a right bestowed upon us by our ancestors. Becoming a victim of the circumstance is a method the weak use to ensure their extinction.

We are learning to think about how we move energy. In so doing, our destiny will change from that of a victim of circumstance to that of a champion of circumstance.

We will not just survive. We will thrive.

We have a decision to make. Make it right now. The decision we make, right now...this moment, will affect the rest of our lives.

We will either decide that our lives will become what we desire them to be, or that we choose to be a victim of circumstance for the rest of our lives.

Choose the right thing.

Part Two

The Nine Laws
and Principles

My Bucket

Psychologists and psychiatrists (as well as biologists, zoologists and many other "ologists" for that matter) tell us that we are a sum of our parts. Our experiences as a baby, youth and young adult go a long way in making us who we are. We view the world through our experiences. The way we react to any exterior stimulus is dictated by all the experiences we have ever had and by how we have been affected by any singular event from our past.

In other words, our lives are nothing more than a bucket of our stuff. The stuff is the collection of all the things we have ever experienced and how it made us feel and think.

That's all in our bucket.

How we view new things that come to us every second is dictated by how similar experiences from our past made us feel and what the consequences were of our actions and reactions at that time. The emotion that was the result of the stimulus and our reaction to that stimulus, combined together, created a judgment. That emotion became imprinted in our brain. Our judgments or emotions or "imprints" dictate how we react to all future, relatively similar stimuli.

Rightly or wrongly, it is a seemingly permanent imprint.

Picture this. The friendly puppy stands in front of us doing his happy dance and wagging his tail so hard we're certain his rear end is going to shake off. He is hoping for some loving because, in his little mind, his cause and effect is that when he does his happy dance, he gets loving.

Our emotion is completely different. We were mauled by a vicious dog as a child. The mere sight of dogs flings us into a terror zone. Our imprint is that of petrification. The little puppy's imprint is that of love. Hopefully, the little puppy's imprint will never change. In order for us to live a full life with the love of a good dog (even when it is someone else's) ours must change. The little puppy's imprint is real, ours isn't. Wait! Stop. Ours **is** real. That's the problem; it exists.

However, it can be changed, which is the whole point here! The little puppy's imprint is real; ours is too. His exists in present time. Ours does not. Well, it does if we insist upon dragging it into present time. Our emotional imprint can be reduced. We can alter our file folder from the past. It is easier than we think.

All the smaller "imprints." We are very capable of washing them away. Stick with me on this….

Some of us are made up of a bucket of crystal clear, pristine water. Some of us have our buckets filled with so much sludge that very little clean water is allowed in and very little sludge will be allowed out. In other words, we are stuck in our sludge…just stuck. Most of us are somewhere in the middle, slogging through the somewhat murky water of our lives, desperately wishing that we could see clearly.

Our conscious mind contains all of the materials that our subconscious mind uses to create both our outer and inner worlds.

It is pretty murky out there, thus in there, therefore out there.

(Ouch…that one gave me a brain cramp.)

The Bucket Analogy

We have two hoses that represent our conscious mind which we control. Through one hose flows pristine water (positive energy), and through the other flows murky water (negative energy). That part is easy to grasp.

In front of us is a five gallon bucket. The inside of the bucket, which represents our subconscious mind, is something we do not control. The outside of the bucket represents our outer and inner world (our life and how we view it).

Directed into the bucket at any given time is one of the hoses. When we put the pristine water hose in our bucket, it begins to fill with good things and the bucket overflows with great things in our lives. When the murky hose is put into our bucket, the same results happen with bad experiences and negative in our lives. These hoses are our conscious mind (something that we control).

Our choice. Our conscious choice. We have control. Simple self-determinism. Period.

Through one of the hoses flows murky water (bad energy). Through the other hose flows crystal clear water (good energy). If we fill the bucket with nothing but dirty water, the bucket (our outer and inner world) overflows with bad experiences. If we fill the bucket with good, pristine water…our experiences will be good and lead us to a great life.

The point is this. We get to choose what we fill our bucket with. We are the ones who choose to fill our lives with nothing but muck…or we can fill our lives with nothing but pristine, clean water. This seems oversimplified and we have all had times when there was nothing but dirty water flooding into the bucket while we frantically searched for the faucet handle.

However, the good news is this. When we choose…when WE choose…we can switch hoses from the murky hose to the pristine hose. Once the crystal clean, pure water is flowing again, cleansing our bucket, we are back on track.

Every now and again something happens that will switch hoses back to the dirty, but the more we practice seeing the signs of this happening, the sooner we switch hoses from the murky water to the pristine hose.

It is simple awareness of which hose is which.

The trick is this. If our bucket is filled with murky water and the murky hose is turned off and we turn the clean hose on, the dirt in our bucket will remain until it has all been flushed out and only the clean is left. We must live through the cleansing of the bucket and not give up while the muck in our bucket is overflowing out.

This is a critical point. To say it again: turning on the pristine water hose does not automatically clean out our bucket. It takes time to flush all the muck out of the bucket. Does a car automatically become clean just because we turn on the garden hose?

Keep the positive flowing and the bucket (our subconscious mind) eventually clears itself. If we keep the positive flow going long enough, there will be no room for our subconscious to hold any more of the dirt (negative).

Remember, the conscious mind is made up of the materials that our subconscious mind uses to create our outer and inner world. The conscious mind we control. The subconscious mind does nothing but create our outer world through the flow of energy which we are putting into the universe.

Our subconscious minds are creating every second, minute and hour of the day. It is imperative that we feed our subconscious minds with the proper materials, the pristine water.

We could have said it a lot more easily with a saying that we have all heard before. The bucket analogy is just a different way to say garbage in, garbage out. Good in, good out.

Fill our mind with good. Start the clean, pristine water. Remember, it is going to take some time to flush out that bucket. Think of how much better our world will look when the bucket is clean.

Focus for a moment. Put the book down and picture your world without your biggest single source of muck. Close your eyes and actually see it.

...Nice smile. You just had a very important realization...an AH-HA moment. We always recognize those moments because the realization makes us smile and sometimes laugh out loud!

Cleansing the bucket creates positive energy. It is not the current stimulus that creates the mud; it is the emotion behind the stimulus that creates what goes into our subconscious minds...our machine, our energy process. Emotions have been locked in from when we were young, from before we had the intellectual capacity to differentiate between thought and emotion.

Imprints

With every stimulus comes an emotion; with every emotion comes a judgment. The emotions range from hurt, pain, sorrow, wonder, joy and happiness to exhilaration. Beneath each emotion there is always and inevitably a judgment. There is no neutral, just judgments that fly lower on our radar screens.

As we are growing up, we form neural pathways through which information (stimulus) is filtered and directed. We are all still "growing up." We are still forming neural pathways. The development of these pathways never stops. We control them.

It is not the intention of these teachings to psychoanalyze all the "blocks" in our lives.

This is key and must be understood. When I have a block in my life, it isn't important to understand all the components of that block, all the "whys" involved. By focusing on all the components of that block, I would continue to keep my focus on negative energy (murky water). By focusing on all the "whys," I continue to keep the murky water flowing into my bucket.

I will acknowledge the block, decide that I am going to change my pathway, and use the lessons taught here to do so. It is enough to realize that I have a block, and that I am working my way toward creating a new neural pathway around it. My new neural pathway will dissipate the negative energy of my previous pathway.

In other words, I acknowledge that there is murky water flowing into my bucket. I choose to turn off the dirty water and take that hose out. I choose to put the clean water hose into my bucket and turn it on. I choose to see every time the hose gets switched back to the dirty water, turn it off again, remove that hose, and put the clear hose back in and turn it on.

When I see that I am making muck, I have had an important realization, and I stop. I am aware. I turn the dirty hose off and turn the pristine on. Full blast.

As a child, and through much of my adult life, I have always been petrified of needles. I had a horrid experience when I was very young when a doctor gave me a shot. It took until well into my adulthood for me to discover that needles weren't bad things. In my young mind, my adverse reaction to the medicine given to me was directly transferred to the needle that gave me the hideous shot.

For decades, the thought of getting a shot, or having my blood drawn, was so scary to me that it caused me to avoid the doctor at all costs, even when I was in agonizing pain or was seriously ill. The imprint had been stamped so hard that it could have killed me. The murky water I had filled my mind with regarding needles had created mud in my bucket that affected my life. This caused my subconscious mind to create a "stop," or block, which negatively affected how I achieved the results I desired.

I unnecessarily continued a painful condition in my life for several years. At wit's end, I went to a doctor who had a pocket full of needles. Through a series of injections, some of them right into my spine, I was greatly healed from the pain I had been experiencing. Imagine that....

For those old enough to know who Norman Rockwell was, picture a drawing of a kid in a hospital gown running down the hall, with a look of horror on their face, being chased by the nurse with the needle in her hand...that was me.

I changed this negative in my life by cleaning this murky water out of my bucket. I consciously told myself that the results of the medical procedures involved in whatever treatment that I undertake will heal me. I created a positive energy around the thought of needles. When I changed the energy around the emotion, it freed me to move on with my life in a way not previously available to me.

Pristine water.

I changed my neural pathway through which I had previously viewed needles by changing the energy around that needle. It is that simple.

This is a very elementary analogy, but it is a useful example. If we think about it, how many people do we know who we think of as "stuck in their ways"? The fact is most of us choose to be this way. Becoming conscious and aware of our past allows us to move on to the present and to switch the hose from the murky to the pristine water.

The most dynamic people we know are those who have made note of why they react to things the way they do and have decided that this is a hindrance to manifesting that which they desire in their lives.

We all have baggage. These lessons are brought to us to help rid us of that baggage. Identifying (acknowledging) a "block" in our lives is crucial in order to change the neural pathway through which a particular stimulus travels. In other words, we see when the murky water gets turned on full blast around certain events in our lives and learn to turn it off and remove that hose from our bucket. We then learn how to get the pristine hose into our bucket and turn that one on. In so doing, we stop the negative energy from flowing into our lives and we turn it to positive energy.

The questions we have in our lives are those around which we will learn to identify and acknowledge the blocks we have created. "Why can't I seem to get ahead?" "Why is my family so messed up?" "Why is it that I cannot find real love?" I don't know what all of our questions are, but we have them. I know what my questions are. I work every day to identify them, and then clear my bucket of the dirty water.

I work every day to identify when I have dirty water flowing into my bucket: I make a conscious decision to turn that hose off; remove it from my bucket; place the hose through which pristine water flows into my bucket; and turn that hose on. Full blast. It is an ongoing process that I shall continue for the rest of my life. What I fill my bucket with, this moment, is what I bring into my future. I am creating every second, minute and hour of the day.

"This is just the way I am." Well, how is it working for you so far?

The point we are all working toward is Truth. Our truth. When our truth lines up with Universal Truth, we will find the peace that God has promised us (Thy will be done, on earth, as it is in heaven). We will be in congruence with the flow of energy through the universe.

Law and Principle # 1

Live in the Now

When one door closes another door opens; but we so often look so long and so regretfully upon the closed door, that we do not see the ones which open for us.
— Alexander Graham Bell

Past. Present. Future. The timelines of our lives. The past is gone. There is nothing we can do to change what has occurred. Yet, the past has a very strong grip on what we do now as well as what we do in the future.

Both what we have learned and how we feel about what we have learned (imprints) dictate the reactions we have to our present situations. This, in turn, gives (compels) a very strong future indication. Thus, our present and future actions are now predictable.

Though the past largely dictates how we react (compulsively) to our current situation, becoming conscious both of what those patterns are and why we react to our world the way we do allows us to control the way we act in our present which, in turn, allows us to control the future.

Become conscious. Let's control our future.

Think of it this way. The present, the "now," is nothing more than a fleeting moment of time. Yet, what we do in this fleeting moment of time controls both our past and future. How we control what we are doing this very second creates and re-creates; it reformats our memories. It also has enormous control over how we act and react in the future. By taking control of the present moment we are wittingly creating our futures.

Start by viewing the worst fear we carry daily. Where did we get it? Let it go, now. It's let go now…or let it go on forever.

I have memories – but only a fool stores his past in the future.
— David Gerrold

When we do the "Now" correctly (positive energy), we don't have to worry about the future, the future happens in a positive way. Plus, we become aware of the treasures of the moment we are living in.

When we live in the present, all that will unfold in our future is being created in this moment.

Energy is in constant motion. The movement of energy is creation. The flow of the universe's energy is moving constantly, being redirected into creation, in every moment throughout time.

The direction of the energy is dictated by our movements in the present. The experiences of the future are determined through the energy we are moving at this moment.

Each law and principle re-determines the movement of energy. We call this movement, through our actions, directed, organized energy.

Orchestrating the nine laws and principles together is directed, organized energy.

Much of our lives are lost worrying about what has happened or what is going to happen. That is living in the past or living in the future. Begin to be aware of thoughts that keep us out of the Now. We can change old patterns.

Choose now to reformulate our pasts. Release its stranglehold from our throats.

There are certain things that keep coming up in our lives. Recognize the issues that keep coming up, that keep holding us back. Whatever the issue is that keeps coming up, it is often a function of forgiveness of ourselves or forgiveness of others.

The more practiced we become at using these principles, the more in the now we are. Being conscious and aware of where our energy is facilitates our living in present time. Consciousness and awareness are the stepping stones of success. This begins the elimination of random, compulsive, disorganized energy.

We cannot change our past actions or erroneous mis-actions, however, we can create our future by what we do right now. Doing the right thing, the right way, right now allows us to let go of "what might happen." By focusing on the present we create predictable abundance in our lives. How do we choose to live our lives?

I am alive right now, right this second. Is the thing I am doing this moment the right thing to do? As my grandfather used to tell me...do the right thing. When I finally asked how we know what the right thing is, he smiled and shook his head (as if he had been waiting for me to ask that question). "The right thing is the one you don't have to think about." Think about that one for a minute. I was pretty young when he imparted his wisdom to me. It took some time to get what he was saying.

It is also called using instinct or intuition.

For now, it is enough to realize I am living in the moment.

Isaiah 43:18-19 Forget the former things; do not dwell on the past. See, I am doing a new thing! Now it springs up; do you not perceive it? I am making a way in the desert and streams in the wasteland. (NIV)

In other words...live right now. Focus on the right now and move positive, directed, organized energy to create the future. When we focus on that which has already happened, we are filling our bucket (subconscious) with the same stuff, which becomes our future reality.

So, what are we filling our buckets with?

This begets the question: what if that which has previously happened was very positive? The answer is when we focus right now on the positive of that thing which had occurred then more positive will happen in the future, as long as that is part of our desired destiny.

"I am doing a new thing." This means I am doing a new thing, right now, which is filling my bucket with good energy. I am doing something new. This is an indicator that I have changed the way I am handling my present situation. I am no longer allowing the past to dictate how I am handling the thing in front of me at this present moment. What I am doing right now is so powerful that it is creating great things (making a way through the desert and streams in the wasteland). Remember, nothing is impossible. We are creating every second, minute and hour of the day.

Do something new. Right now. Start with a smile. Decide that we are going to be happy today. (What a novel concept, simply deciding that we are going to be happy today....)

The fact is we cannot change the past. However, in certain ways, we have control over the past. When we control the moment we are living in, we have taken over our past. We have the ability and grace to forgive our past. By living in the now we are creating our future as we choose, a good future, which will become our past. Do the now correctly and the past will happen in a very positive way.

Forgive our past. Let it go. Every time it comes up to bite us, turn and confront its action; laugh at it and say that we no longer do that. We choose not to. A habit is only an uncontrollable reaction until we take control of it.

By doing the now the right way, we are creating our future, which will become our past, which we will view in a favorable way.

Don't let the past steal your present. — Terri Guillemets

Grasp this moment, this very moment...and do something great with it.

I am tomorrow, or some future day, what I establish today. I am today what I established yesterday or some previous day.
— James Joyce

We will see this principle, living in the now, in the remainder of the points made. Remember this. The way I am at any given moment is changing history. I am choosing to change history for the better right now as I type this.

This does not mean that we don't make plans, set agendas and create goals. We do. When we are creating them, we are living in the moment.

I was in a seminar once when the facilitator was speaking about how he plans his week, month, year, etc. He told us how he operated his day as he always did, writing new things into his calendar while performing the responsibilities of the moment. He told of how easy it was. He was creating his future, now. All he had to do was be present. This is a prime example of living in the moment. The future took care of itself.

All he had to do was show up.

How are we creating our day? How are we creating our future? Do we always show up? Always?

Create the map. Design the future. When we create goals in the now, using pristine water, we create our pristine future...now.

Ask this question: Am I present in this moment? Am I here, focused on what it is that I am doing at this present time?

No yesterdays are ever wasted for those who give themselves to today. — Brendan Francis

Do what we are doing when we are doing it. Focus.

Years ago, there was a book written about sports mentality and focusing called *The Inner Game of Tennis* by Tim Gallwey. To paraphrase, the book talked about the trust between the mind and the body. After years of training to hit a tennis ball, why is it that the mind can take control of the game and throw off the way one plays? When we take judgment out of the game (tennis, skiing, life, work, whatever the game is), and become observant of how our body reacts to a certain stimulus within our lives, we are able to discover what it is that brings us to peak performance, without judgment, and without worry.

Taking judgment away means eliminating the past (imprints) from the current actions (the now). It also means taking judgment of potential consequences of the future away from the current actions. This allows our bodies to perform actions without the hindrance of the "what ifs." It allows us to perform at our peak potential.

By taking the judgment away, we learn to watch the way the various aspects of our lives affect our emotions. It also becomes clearer where the emotions are coming from. At that point we become more proactive in being able to acknowledge the emotion for what it is, and to decide to move beyond it. Self-doubt and anxiety are obstacles that hinder our daily performance in any task we set out to do (or not do). Allowing ourselves to perform without the doubt and anxiety allows us to do what comes naturally, at our highest level.

The inner game is about knowing how to get out of our own way and let our best game emerge. It is a matter of trusting ourselves and playing the game the best we know how. The lapses of concentration come from self-doubt, nervousness and anxiety. Let's let go of those and just allow ourselves only positive thoughts. As soon as the negative thoughts appear, immediately replace all of them with positive ones completely focused upon the present moment.

Those Olympic golden moments are the ones free of inappropriate (past) emotions. They shine as the moments when all we are doing is this one correct (present) action. No mud. No mis-emotion. Only directed emotion and pristine water.

Just skiing this hill. Just hitting this ball. Just finishing the report. Just loving our child. Just playing ball with our children. Just rapidly bagging the groceries. Just being fully aware of the conversation we are having. Just reading this line. (Are we somewhere else right now? Come back.)

Are those nagging emotions helping us with our life at this very moment? Stop feeding them attention.

Stop judging by some outside standard. This relieves a great deal of anxiety in our life. Everything we do should be measured (without judgment) by our own standards. When it is time to sit down and analyze to improve our performance, everything we do should meet with one question. How could I do this better? I don't ask this of myself to meet anyone else's standards, just mine.

Taking ourselves out of the "blame game" allows us to view the current event in a way not previously available. When our peak performance is not at the level we desire it to be, we see the things that we wish to improve and, without judgment, decide what actions are necessary to improve them.

This allows us to play the game (life) to the best of our ability and takes the focus away from that which is outside of our control. This also facilitates bypassing our ego and allows us to do what it is that we know how to do. When we put the ego away, when we visualize what we wish to get done or where we desire to get to, it is far more easily accomplished.

Telling our mind to be quiet does not work (negative). Arguing with ourselves does not work (negative). What works is focusing on the moment we are in, on the task at hand. In so doing, we observe our behavior, without judgment, in order to correct that action which does not serve us in accomplishing our goal. Our attention is only on those aspects of a situation that are required to accomplish the task at hand.

My son and daughter were ski racers. Both were fairly accomplished at their levels. Rachael is 18 months older than Sean.

I overheard them lamenting one day about how they could not even begin to master a drill that the coach was instructing them to do. I watched as they struggled through the rest of the drills that day. Both came back to the cabin at the end of the day somewhat dejected. I asked how I could help.

They both explained that they knew what the coach was asking, and Rachael expressed how she "knew if she set up her turn in the way that the coach requested, she would not be in the right position for the next turn." Sean told me that if he did what the coach asked he would be going too fast to make the next turn.

They were making judgments based on past, or old, information and the results they were experiencing were exactly what they thought they would be.

That night one of the younger coaches stopped by the cabin to say hi and talk to the kids. Here were her total instructions: "Tomorrow, right before you start down the course, you are going to put your favorite song in your head and hear it clearly as you push off onto the course." (No iPods, just the music in their heads.)

The next day Rachael went through her first run having forgotten about the coach's instructions. Her results were about the same. When she got to the bottom, the coach did not ridicule, instruct or judge. All she did was ask Rachael what song was going through her head. Rachael smiled, said nothing and raced off for the chairlift for her next run. On her next run she took a full second and a half off her time...in ski racing that is an eternity.

That afternoon Sean came skiing up to me with the biggest grin on his face. I asked him how he had done. With a laugh he told me that he had crashed and burned on his second run..."But Mom, I have never, ever skied that fast on a course...I really get it now. I can't wait for the next run." Today he was having fun; yesterday was not so fun.

What changed? Their focus. They had each gotten "out of their own heads." They each had gotten out of their own way. By listening to the tune playing in their heads, they removed the past judgments and all the "what ifs" of their future. It allowed their bodies to perform to the highest possible level. They experienced joy living in the moment.

It is time to get out of our own way.

With the past, I have nothing to do; nor with the future. I live now.
— Ralph Waldo Emerson

This "living in the now," this "just let go of the past and do the now" handles more of our past baggage that we are dragging around than we would think. It works for the majority of our carry-ons and baggage. We will address the heavier luggage with additional methods further on in the Invisible Truth. For now, just start knocking over as many suitcases as possible by living in the now. Make some mental room for the next laws and principles.

Create our first affirmation right now: I live in the now. I am performing this moment in my life to the very best of my ability.

In renowned Dr. Carl Jung's opinion on unresolved emotions and the idea of Karma: *"when an inner situation is not made conscious, it appears outside as fate."* [1]

Read that quote again. Stop for a minute and think about what Dr. Jung was saying here. If we are not conscious of what we are doing in this present moment, what happens to us because of our lack of consciousness appears to have been our fate. The key word here is "appears." In other words, whatever has happened to us, we just let it happen. Then we lamented that there was nothing that we could have done about it because it was meant to be; it was our fate.

Is our life running us? Or are we running our life?

Finish each day and be done with it. You have done what you could; some blunders and absurdities have crept in; forget them as soon as you can. Tomorrow is a new day; you shall begin it serenely and with too high a spirit to be encumbered with your old nonsense. — Ralph Waldo Emerson

Be conscious and aware of this moment. Move energy in a positive way. Live in the now. We will find this principle laced throughout the remainder of the lessons. Let's move forward.

Matthew 6:34 Therefore do not worry about tomorrow, for tomorrow will worry about itself. (NIV)

Restated using, instead, the laws of the universe we say this: When we do the now correctly, the future happens in a positive way.

If you are still talking about what you did yesterday, you haven't done much today. — Unknown

Action Steps for the Week

- Write down our goals for the day. Take five minutes.

- Decide which on our list we will perform first.

- Perform all the tasks necessary to accomplish that task. Focus only on that task.

- When that task is completed, move to the next task.

- If something crucial comes up while we are doing what is necessary to finish the task, do what the moment requires of us and then get back to the task at hand until it is complete.

- Choose our next task. Repeat.

Law and Principle # 2

Thoughts

As a single footstep will not make a path on the earth, so a single thought will not make a pathway in the mind. To make a deep physical path, we walk again and again. To make a deep mental path, we must think over and over the kind of thoughts we wish to dominate our lives. — Henry David Thoreau

Thought is energy. Energy is in constant motion. We bring things into our lives that vibrate at the same magnitude as our thoughts. Therefore, if our thoughts vibrate at lower (negative) levels, we bring things to us that vibrate at those same levels. By thinking higher (positive) level thoughts, we attract higher level vibrations (things and people) to us.

Besides that, it is just a lot easier, and more fun, to think good, clean, happy, positive thoughts.

Many Eastern traditions base their healthcare and healing on the subtle pulse (vibration) of the human body. The vibration we carry throughout our bodies is heavily influenced by the energy of our thought.

You are today where your thoughts have brought you; you will be tomorrow where your thoughts take you. — James Allen

When we are by ourselves, driving down the road, doing the dishes, whatever we are doing on auto-pilot, we are thinking.

Usually we are thinking about things from the past or dreams of our future.

"If I had only smiled when my boss talked to me today, he would have calmed down," or "I wish I could have yelled at that evil guy who cut me off today," or "I really don't know what to make of what my wife told me today...I wonder if she is straying or is unhappy with our marriage," or...we do it constantly. We take these thoughts back to our earliest childhood at the slightest provocation. "They are always mean to me." It goes on and on. Slights. Hurts. Injustices. They come to us randomly. Random, compulsive and disorganized energy. This is the murky water running into our bucket which overflows into our lives.

We could just as easily be thinking of the positives in our lives. There was that time when I got an "A" on my assignment that I didn't expect, or the time I scored that touchdown, or when Mom and Dad bought me the Christmas present I was really excited about. We have a tendency to overlook these moments.

Sometimes, maybe just as often, thoughts of the future invade our minds.

"Man, I got all these bills to pay...I don't know how I am going to do it. I don't think I can. The stress is killing me," or "I hope I don't get laid off my job. I would lose the house and what will we do then?" or "I really don't feel like going to work today. I am so depressed. I think I will just call in sick," or "What's going to happen tomorrow because of what I did today?" We get the picture. We have all been there.

By simply becoming aware of the thoughts we are having...by being conscious of how we think...we begin the process of changing our thought processes.

Time for a change. Now.

Freedom to, Not Freedom from

We are free to choose the life we desire, given the rules for living in a herd. By realizing I am free to create my world, I have taken the first step in creating my destiny, and not just allowing fate to create my life.

By understanding that we are each free to create our life, we are creating positive energy in our world, which attracts like kind energy. By seeking "freedom from," we keep the focus on what it is that we "want freedom from." In other words, if we keep our focus on that which we desire to escape, we never will.

Freedom is doing what we desire. Not doing that which we wish to be "free from" is not freedom at all. It is focusing on the negative, thereby bringing more of the same into our lives.

Janis Joplin sang to us the words of Kris Kristofferson... "Freedom's just another word for nothing left to lose." The converse is also true. Freedom is just another word for everything to gain.

Hoping to escape certain patterns we have created in our lives creates and keeps a focus on those problems.

It also creates a jumble of thoughts about the problem and the consequences of that problem. These are the random, continuous, compulsive thoughts that keep invading our minds. The murky hose is on full blast.

These thoughts wreak havoc in our lives. They create self-infliction, illness, suffering and fear. All of these are detrimental to us. In some cases they can contribute to fatal illness.

They create The Victim Mentality. They create The Martyr. They create the "Can't you see how hard I try?" mentality.

Such as are your habitual thoughts; such also will be the character of your mind; for the soul is dyed by the color of your thoughts.
— Marcus Aurelius, Roman Emperor

Mental health professionals have focused their study of humans on mental illness. They have focused their attention on "getting to the bottom" of the issue. In some cases, this is a very valid approach.

However, true mental illness often has a physiological cause. Brain development in the womb, or after birth, is slightly (or severely) altered from that of "normal" brains. In other words, there is a true physical reason why the brain works in certain ways. Also, mental and emotional disorders are often a sociological consequence of life experiences. Sometimes they are a consequence of one's physical environment. This book is not an authority on mental or emotional illnesses or disorders. Most of us do not suffer from these.

We have just lost our way.

We have created minor mental and emotional disorders which we process on a daily basis, however, there is nothing physically wrong with us. Sometimes there is something physically wrong with us due to the environment we have created. When our body chemistry is out of balance, it affects our mental and emotional processes.

One way or the other, we are caught in the random, compulsive thoughts that take us where we don't desire to be. At times we regurgitate the "issues" over and over again, and keep the focus on the negative, as we strive to "get to the bottom of it." Remember, the movement of energy is creation. The energy we move right now is our future; we are creating it right this very second.

Keep in mind that what we fill our buckets with now is attracted back to us at the same vibration. As we progress, we process these thought patterns in a way that manifests that which we choose, instead of "dealing with the world" as a reaction. Our directed, organized thoughts will create action instead of random, disorganized reaction.

When we acknowledge the "issues" we become aware of our thoughts going into our buckets, therefore we control them. We are going towards the light instead of continuing to run around in the muck. We are using the pristine hose.

When the same issue persisting in holding our attention, we attract to us the same vibrational energy that we are putting into these thoughts.

For example, if my best friend is upset with me over a real or perceived slight, and I have apologized with no result, awareness of the situation within my thoughts is key. Questions must be asked of myself: "Is what I am thinking about the situation real? Am I living in the now? What am I filling my bucket with? What is my intention? Is my intention clean? Are the words I used consistent with my intention? Was the apology to my friend sincere? Have I forgiven myself? Are there previous unresolved issues or am I living in the now? Is resolving past issues necessary in order to move forward with the unconditional love of my friend?"

We are learning to create new neural pathways through which we process the events and energy in our lives, thereby giving us new ways to perceive the world.

Sometimes it takes professional help to "get to the bottom of it." But, when we have that AH-HA moment, head straight back toward the light. With awareness comes the opportunity to change a negative to a positive. Remember what we focus on is what we create. We are not required to muddle around in the mud forever. Muddling around in the mud keeps the body and soul in the darkness. We are looking for physical change, not just mental and emotional change.

Test out utilizing directed, organized energy. Right now. Let's use directed, controlled, organized energy in our thoughts regarding our own health. What do we think causes our dis-ease? Who allowed it? We did. Time to change thought patterns. It is time to control the way we think.

I lost you for a minute. Come back. Put the book down for a moment. Consider who or what is causing random, compulsive, disorganized energy within you right now. Change the pattern. Be conscious of the method by which you judge whatever energy comes at you.

By mastering the energy in our lives, we are eroding our disorder. Erosion of disorder leads to control. We master the energy in our lives by controlling our thoughts. This is movement towards the light.

How does your energy look right now?
Darkness causes disease. Dis...ease. Not at ease. Confusion, anger, hatred, bad attitude...cause disease and death. Dis-ease of one or more parts of the body's systems. Disorder.

Opening Pandora's box is essential. For some, it's a scary thing. When I open the box I have kept tightly closed for my entire life and dare to peer at its contents, I am facing my biggest, darkest secrets. My deepest, darkest fears. It is these fears that I have been running from...*trying* to get as much distance between "them" and me as possible. Guess what? Didn't happen, did it? Seems like they are tied to my back belt loop. Every time I look over my shoulder, they are right behind me.

I am no longer going to seek freedom from these boogey men from the dark past. Now, I choose to look squarely at them and make peace with them.

Most of the life events that keep us from moving forward are so mundane that the second we acknowledge them, they disappear. Some of them require more work.

Some don't vanish the moment we confront them head-on. With those, we must peer into the darkness to see the secret we are hiding from ourselves there in the closet. It is most frequently unclaimed guilt hidden there in the darkness. Tell ourselves the unacknowledged truth. Accept it.

See the life event for what it is. Acknowledge it. Turn on the pristine hose. Now, let the mis-emotion go.

Everyone avoids pain. This is a basic human instinct. However, when not looking at that painful moment in our life keeps us from achieving our dream, then it is time to confront it head-on. I dare say...make friends with it. Only then will we gain the freedom to achieve our goals, and not stumble around "trying" to be free from that dark pain.

Our boogey men aren't any different, any more or less scary than the ones inside the guy standing next to us. To think that we are alone with our demons is a bit egotistical, don't you think? As the good pastor said in one of the sermons I attended, "Yours is the worst experience I have ever heard...except for everybody else's."

If professional counseling is our chosen option, then so be it. If finding a trusted friend to tell is the ticket, that is fine too. (But be sure that we ask permission and let them know our intent. By letting them know our intent, we are giving them permission to view our baggage as just that...baggage. They are a lot less likely to take the baggage on themselves.)

If workshops are the thing to do, there are plenty out there that will let us take a good hard look at our stuff and help us get through it. Our choice: join a support group, build a friendship circle, or find a hobby group.

If all it takes is us deciding that we know who the boogey man is and that we are going to take him on ourselves...good for us. Just do it.

Creating the Freedom to

The best way to control these thoughts (random, compulsive, disorganized energy) is to simply be aware of them. Once we become aware of these thoughts, we can control them and consciously change them. We can turn the clean water on and the murky water off.

Become aware.

At times our bucket is so full of murky water, it seems difficult, if not impossible, to change these habitual thought patterns. Remember, the bucket does not become clean automatically. It takes some time. Becoming aware of our thoughts, all the time, is the first step in cleaning out our bucket. It is up to us. If we wish to change, then we shall just do it.

Change is not easy…or is it? Once we become aware that we are on autopilot most of the time, we realize the mechanisms necessary to take it off autopilot and look at the world with new eyes. When we have done that, change becomes easy. If we desire it, then we shall just do it.

Look at it. See it for what it is. It is mud. Turn off the murky water. Right now. Remove the dirty hose. Place the clean hose into our bucket. Turn it on. Change a negative to a positive. This requires work, which we cover in law and principle five, *Work*. However, practice does make perfect.

Our spirit, our soul, thrives on goodness and light. It is so easy to get caught in the darkness. Come out of the darkness into the light. It is a lot more fun here in the light.

Freedom to…not freedom from.

Perfection is born of practice. Let's change a few of our "freedom from" habitual thoughts to "freedom to" now. Freedom to is the concept of that which we strive for. Freedom from is that which we wish to avoid.

Focus on that which we are…that which we desire; keep our eye on the target. As my dad used to say, "Keep your eye on the doughnut, not on the hole."

Freedom from that which we choose to avoid is not freedom at all. It keeps the focus on what we do not desire.

"I have healthy lungs," which is a positive energy, puts the focus on how healthy our lungs are. "I am a non-smoker" means that we are focusing on what we don't wish to do…keeping the focus on smoking (or not smoking…a negative energy). "I love being in shape; I feel good (a positive energy)." "I like working out, I like working out, I like working out." (Okay, some are harder than others.) "I've paid all my bills (though admirable and necessary…a negative energy)." "I am creating more money all of the time; it flows easily to me (a positive energy)." Positive draws in positive.

Thoughts become things. — Mike Dooley

Discipline

Changing our thoughts requires discipline. A lifetime of discipline. The lazy will choose to allow their mind to drift wherever it takes them. The disciplined are aware of what they are thinking, control where their minds take them, and create solutions rather than dwell on the problems.

Definitively choose a solution that grants us ultimate happiness.

The most common erroneous set of beliefs is quite familiar to us all. The victim mentality is an exhausting, disabling and debilitating mindset. A positive, possibility mentality is one that allows for greatness. It takes practice and rewiring of the brain. It starts with awareness. Becoming aware is key to beginning a new way to think about things.

Awareness requires discipline. Discipline requires awareness.

Understanding Our Power

We are powerful beyond measure. We have the power to change the energy in the universe in a positive way. We are an instrument of change…realize it and accept it.

Every negative thought that goes through our head drains our power. Every time somebody says something that is of no real consequence to us and we allow it to negatively affect us, we lose more power. Every time something happens that is of no real consequence, and we dwell on the negative of the situation, our battery gets sucked dry.

> *No one can make you feel inferior without your consent.*
> — Eleanor Roosevelt

Most of the time we simply allow it to happen.

When we begin to realize and accept that we are exactly what we have created...when we take full responsibility for our life...we begin to take our power back. We are no longer a victim. We have become the champion of our own cause...us. It is time to allow our power to be on at all times.

Once we have taken responsibility for our life, and we own that responsibility, there is no reason to get or be defensive anymore. Whatever it is that comes to our minds through thought or words...we simply acknowledge as being the truth (or not) of the situation. There is no longer a need to rationalize or justify.

Our stance has changed.

By no longer being defensive, we have taken all the virility of the "attack" out of the thing we are confronting. Rationalization and justification are the actions that cause our bodies to tense up, and our minds to go into a defensive posture, ready to do battle.

By definition, a fight requires a minimum of two combatants. What if we didn't show up? That does not mean we are a "chicken." It just means that we have no need to do battle. That is called "staying in our power."

Of all the martial artists I know, to a person, none have ever used their fighting skill in combat. They are prepared...but, because

they know how to do battle, they feel no need to participate.
Usually they are the biggest peacekeepers.

Think about the people who are in our lives. Some of them are real
downers and we dread seeing them or being around them. There is
always something wrong in their life. They seem to suck the life
right out of us. We know the ones we're talking about. Funny thing
is...we allow it.

Some people are delightful bundles of conscious energy whom we
look forward to being around. We are uplifted when we feel their
energy. They always have a kind word, a gentle touch. We just feel
better being around them. That is great power.

Ask ourselves who would we rather be like?

Find that person right now. Envision them. The sound of their
voice makes us smile. Hearing their laughter brings a giggle of our
own.

I am smiling as I write this, picturing my adored grandfather.
Smiling...he sometimes called me "stinky"...with his gruff, little
chuckle (like he was pulling one over on you). Oh, how I loved the
man. He always had a kind word and a warm thought. He has not
been on this earth for several decades, but I see him and feel him
like it was yesterday.

Then, there are the folks at the coffee shop I stop at every morning.
Part of the reason I go there is because the shopkeeper and his
helpers are always quick with a smile and a joke or a kind word.
The shopkeeper is often singing along with some song that is
playing in the store. He makes me smile. Even when it is out of my
way, I will stop in there just to say hi and to share a smile.

Power also runs the other direction. All of us have, on occasion,
been the power mongers who felt it necessary to suck the life out
of another. We do it with intent, often rationalizing our actions as
being justified given the circumstance or situation. It's not. Be
nice.

Don't allow our power to be drained from us and don't give it away. At the same time, don't take it from others...it leads to bad karma.

Patterns

The negative patterns we can fall into are not set in stone for the rest of our life. We can break free; it is never too late. It starts with becoming aware of what we are actually saying to ourselves.

Listen...it makes for some intriguing thoughts.

I am always shocked at how rapidly the murky water can fill my bucket. Now I recognize this pattern and can change it. As I do this, I am developing a new pathway.

Even those who think they are the most positive type of person, the more they start listening to themselves, the more they realize how often their thoughts create doubt, fear, anxiety and stress. The more aware one becomes of their thoughts, the easier it is to change those thought patterns.

The more we practice our new thought patterns, the more permanent the change becomes.

With permanent change comes a whole new way to look at the world. Joy and happiness come with our thoughts. The bucket is becoming clean. It is possible. All we have to do is choose it. The more we practice, the more accelerated success becomes.

Become aware. Turn the pristine hose on. Again and again and again.

My Change

Some time ago, when it seemed that my world was crashing in on me, I realized that it was my perception of the world that required changing. My mom had recently died. I was in the process of potentially losing my business, and had decided to split from my spouse. To add insult to injury, the illness I had carried with me for so many years decided to come back, full force. I was flat on my back. It seemed I could not get off the couch.

The change began by my acknowledging the importance of my mother in my life. I saw her as she was, enveloped in all of the help and love she gave me, not the cancer-ridden woman of the last few months. I began to hear her laugh and feel her sweet touch on my children.

I got up off the couch. I became determined that I was going to find a way to heal from my illness. I started my journey in Colorado with Reverend Hanna Kroeger. She showed me self-healing techniques by teaching me how to determine what method, product or procedure best facilitated the body to heal itself. Her biggest passion was helping others help themselves through knowledge. She stressed the importance of learning to tap into each individual's healing power. She taught cooperation with nature and harmony with God's miracle foods. I am blessed to have met her.

My new thought process took me from being someone in dread to becoming a seeker. As I wove my way through the world of homeopathy, I met some wonderful people who changed my life. It was then that I decided that this was the world I was going to create for myself and make a good living doing it.

I also began to see the world around belief and energy. More than the food that I put into my body, it was also the energy around how I was thinking. If we follow a natural holistic path and feed our bodies proper nutrition, yet our minds dwell on the negative diagnosis the doctor left us with, we live in contradiction.

From deep within, from the very core of my being, with every waking thought, I chose to heal.

The treatment being offered by my medical doctor was not a viable option to me. With a success rate of five percent, combined with unacceptable side effects, I chose to look elsewhere. I chose to find my own path. I strove to heal in a way that was driven, no matter how long it took. I am succeeding. With "the faith of a mustard seed," I moved "the mountain" of the western medical community out of my path and found my own path to health and wellness.

I set my mind to the task of finding wellness. With faith, I continue to find it every day.

Freedom to...not freedom from.

Miracles: the only difference between faith and science.
— Theresa Wyne

In order for the wonderful nutrition we are feeding ourselves to work, we must also have a healthy mindset.

I changed my thoughts. I changed my energy. I am making a living doing what I love to do, and helping people at the same time. But, oh boy, what an adventure it has been. I wouldn't trade it for the world. Having come from the darkness, I can truly appreciate the light.

Many see this as the hardest part to conquer in behavioral change. Some dismiss this entire concept because "it is impossible to change a leopard's spots." Remember, this is a lifelong process. Some behavior and thought patterns do not change the second I decide that I am going to change them.

It happens when we make a commitment to "change our lot in life." It starts when I commit to changing my life, to always striving toward the positive, right thought. I know the difference. Each of us does. It comes back to what we learned when we were small children. We know the difference between right and wrong. The wrong thing is the one we have to think about. The one we have to justify.

It is okay to change. It is okay to strive to be a better human being. Life is full of stepping stones. One step at a time.

"Well…it's just the way I am." Well…how's it working for you so far?

The Laws of Attraction (Creation)

There are so many studies on the Laws of Attraction, so much scientific data that it seems redundant to even cite any of them here. Remember the old adage "Be careful what you wish for"? It is not an old wives' tale. The Laws of Attraction (Creation) bring us what we ask for. Be mindful of what we ask for, especially if we're on autopilot.

One of the conclusions of the scientific community is that negative energy vibrates at a much lower level than positive energy. This means that lower levels of vibration do not attract at the same rate as higher (positive) levels of vibration. Logic dictates that positive energy (thought) attracts at a much greater (faster) rate than negative energy (thought).

The solution lies within us. It is human nature to dwell on the negative. That is just the way it is when we are lazy and not disciplined…or aware. Stop the negative. Instead, install the best set of thoughts that can come from the circumstance. How I react to any given situation is a direct reflection on how I live.

We have all laughed at A.A. Milne's *Winnie the Pooh* character, Eeyore. The reason we like Eeyore is because we can relate to the character. Stop being Eeyore! We no longer relate to Eeyore. Pick another character. Be Tigger. (Every time I think of that character, I can't help but spell out his name…T…I…double Gah…ER…Tigger.)

Now, that does not mean that we are phonies. Nothing is worse than inappropriate pervasive enthusiasm. That is a falsehood that is grating on even the most patient of people. What I choose in my life is to see the best of any given situation, to see the results I choose in any circumstance, and to put my best foot forward in achieving those results.

Besides that, choosing to be a happy positive person is so much more fun than choosing to be anguished, despondent or melancholy.

Another old saying and a good one to remember is "Will my negative thoughts allow me to live one day longer?"

Well, will they?

It is a fact that negative thoughts do just the opposite and bring death prematurely.

I remember an older neighbor of mine from when I was growing up. He was always the positive type of guy who I liked to be around. The apple didn't fall far from the tree. His mother was something else again. What a bundle of energy she was. At 75 years old, she often told her son that she "had to put him on her calendar" for lunch or a visit. An effervescent personality if ever there was one.

When she was diagnosed with cancer, her response was…"Oh, I simply don't have time for this. My calendar is full for the next five years." Well, the doctors' prognosis and timeline for her did not fit her schedule. The medical community gave her a year, maybe two, tops. The old gal finished her schedule, and when she decided it was her time, she went to her reward.

I reiterate…she decided….

Freedom to…not freedom from.

Remember, what we focus on is what comes clear in our life. If I am reading a book, I can see all that is on the page I am reading. I cannot see what is on the next page because I am focused on the current one. I am not worried about the next page. I will get there. My focus is here. Right here on this page. The next page will result on its own.

Focus. Be in the present. Do the now, now. Do what we are doing while we are doing it. Keep our thoughts on the present moment and what we are doing now.

When it is time to think about other things, think about them. When it is time to dream, dream BIG.

Be conscious of what we are thinking and how what we are thinking is affecting us.

Thought is the blossom; language the bud; action the fruit behind it. — Ralph Waldo Emerson

The vibration of what we are thinking is what is attracted right back to us. If I am focused on what the boss said to me today, if it was a negative situation and I am dwelling on it, there is a very good chance that I am going to get more of the same. If I focus on the negative energy, I attract more negative energy.

That is not a principle. That is a law.

When I fill my bucket continuously with murky water, it is soon going to be overflowing with the same and it becomes more difficult to stem the tide. I will keep getting murky water in my life. Is that what I choose? If not, then I will become aware of my thoughts, turn the murky water off and start filling my bucket with pristine water.

The murky water overflowing my bucket often comes out in the form of pessimistic talk. While we are saying these negative things, we are reinforcing them in our psyche. It is a vicious circle that requires awareness and the changing of an old neural pathway in order to move forward into the light.

Awareness.

Think of how we feel when we are listening to a negative person. Unless we are conscious of what is going on, we end up sinking right to their level. They're angry; we get angry. They're grumbling about some nothingness; we start grumbling. They're crying; with empathy, we feel like crying. They're always dejected, so we become discouraged. They're apathetic and inconsolable, so we start feeling slower, more tired, and much more morose. Our life begins to seem heavier and harder. Our life feels wretched because their burden is challenging and they have a chronic, low-toned attitude.

Plus, they have only problems, never solutions.

Is it time to reevaluate this "friendship"? Do we really require that negative friendship just to keep ourselves free from the vast boredom of our own humdrum lives alone?

In order to live free and happily, you must sacrifice boredom. It is not always an easy sacrifice. — Richard Bach

Do we see the negative energy patterns in our lives? We are now aware of them.

When that thought of what the boss said comes to mind, become aware of the feelings around that thought and change them. Create a positive response. If it is an issue we have to deal with, deal with it in a positive approach. Create. Change it into something good.

Instead of thinking, "I wish he'd leave me alone," think, "I am creating a great spreadsheet for us."

Let's say I was late getting a vital report in. The boss thought it critical to the proposal he was compiling for his boss. If I dwell on his reprimand, the negative vibration will stick with me. If I focus on why the report was late, decipher the cause, and then determine how to prevent this misunderstanding in the future, I have moved toward the positive. That may not be apparent at first.

Instead of thinking, "I'm such a failure. I wish I didn't keep messing up," say, "I'm coming in early every day this week to make the next report perfect." Then do it.

Solutions...not problems.

You're either part of the solution or part of the problem.
— Eldridge Cleaver

What I determine I will do next time is clarify the assignment, seek help, or explain why I require assistance on the assignment. This takes me from a negative vibration mode to a positive vibration mode. It takes me from reaction to creation. It also allows assistance to come into my life. It is human nature to help. All we have to do is ask for it and help comes.

It is also critical to understand that, when given the troublesome assignment, if I knew the boss's timeframe was impossible, then that was the time to speak up. In fact, it is my responsibility to speak up. Otherwise, I am setting myself up for failure. ("But, can't you see how hard I am trying?") Saying no is the right thing to do at times.

In this case there may be extenuating circumstances, so no matter how reasonable the assignment, I know I will not be able to accomplish it in the desired time frame. Do not confuse this issue and use it as an excuse for every time there is something challenging coming towards us.

Avoidance is another negative.

The consequence of not getting the assignment done is a stepping stone. Bringing (our) truth to the table best serves all involved. Telling ourselves and others around us the truth is the best way to avoid the victim thing.

No one is intentionally setting us up to fail. If they are, it is essential to see that and bring the truth to light at the time it is occurring.

Understanding the task is critical. Understanding the point of the task is also crucial. Once these things are clear, the timeline must be understood. At that point, the probabilities of completing the assignment on time will become clear.

We are now armed with knowing what we don't know. If what we don't know can be answered by others, it is time to ask for help. This may require explaining why we are seeking help as others require understanding also. When the assignment is understood, it will be accomplished.

Manifest. "With the help of others, I am becoming the best report writer in the office."

It is an amazing thing, and surely one of the best hopes for mankind. People love to help.

Thought is action in rehearsal. — Sigmund Freud

There is a fine line here. There are no masters, only students. Just keep going.

Change It to Positive

Live in the now. Think and focus on the now. When we think and focus on the past, we create those things in our future. We bring those things into our future. What we fill our buckets up with now is what overflows in the future. It only makes sense to "do the now… now." If we stay in the now and "do the now" correctly, we don't have to worry about the future, the future will result in a very positive way.

My idle time used to be lying in bed readying myself to sleep or in the morning after I had awoken and before I got up. These were the times I was most apt to dwell on things, most commonly on negative things. It was then when I would realize I forgot to do something the day before or would think about an incident that had happened the day before, week before, year before, or years ago, that negatively affected my life.

Sometimes I used to just lie in bed apprehensive of the day because of one worry or another. That led to dread, depression and negativity. The puny faux pas of yesterday generally hurled me straight back to my humiliation of a long ago incident that had nothing to do with the current circumstance.

Instead of beating myself up, yet again, I could have chosen to take a deep breath to summon up the courage to apologize to my friend today for my misspoken words or my inconsiderate actions. It would have been easier on my heart. I would have risen smiling, full of tenacity.

Now, I have changed that. I can't wait to get out of bed in the morning. (Well, that isn't entirely true. I can't wait for the day, but I do love my sleep. With a clear conscience, I have the most wonderful dreams!) And I have no trouble falling asleep the night before. I have consciously done all that I chose to do with my day to move the energy to get myself advancing toward my goals. If there was something that I had forgotten the day before, and it was important, I decide that I will clear the issue at my first opportunity and deal with whatever ramifications there are as I go. I do not ignore the situation.

If the thought that comes to my mind is of something that happened some time ago, say, the death of a loved one and the pain it caused…I change my thought to something positive about that person. Like my grandfather. Just thinking of him now, and writing this, makes me smile. When I think about my mom, it may start with a shot of pain, but then I start to think about her wonderful sense of humor…and often I will get up laughing. I think of all the joy there was in the house when my daughter, her first grandchild, was born. Oh, those memories I cherish. They make me smile.

Take a moment for ourselves, right now. Think of something that has brought and continues to bring us pain. The death of a loved one. A car accident. A necessary surgery. A divorce.

Whatever it is, envision it right now. Feel all of the pain. Feel it. See it. All of it. Understand it. Release any mis-emotion.

Acknowledge it for what it actually is without the judgment wrapped around the emotion of the incident.

Now, find the positive in the incident or person. If it is of a loved one passing, recall the joyous moments spent with that loved one. Think of one time with that person that brought laughter. Feel the joy as it was then. Focus on it. Bring that person back and feel all of the positive they caused in life.

Stay there in that moment of positive energy. Bask in it. Revel in that emotion we have deprived ourselves of. Congratulations. We have just created a new neural pathway.

Okay, moving forward. Granted, there are things that happen in our life that it is a real stretch to put a positive on. That car accident that nearly killed us would be a tough one for anybody. However, there is a positive there. There was the physical therapist we met while going through rehab. Then, there was the upbeat friend we made who encouraged us through it. Maybe it was discovering who our real friends were as we were recovering.

I am going to get up out of this bed and do a little dance. I may wobble a lot at first, and someone may have to hold me up a time or two, but a jig it shall be. Sing me a tune and I will do it.

That surgery I had? I find it impressive that technology of today had a method by which to make me better. I get to brag about experiencing the technology. I am healthy now because of the surgery. The surgery was a success. It might hurt a bit now, but the results are going to be great. What…people would like me to start dancing again? Be happy, too!

The woman or man we divorced…we married them for a reason. Things may not have worked out, but we married them for a valid reason. Focus on that. Focus on the wonderful children we brought into the world together. Focus on the positive. Think of the love we shared. Be grateful for that love. It was good.

Focus on the positive. Luxuriate in it; it is ours. Freedom to…!

When a thought that we do not choose to put into our bucket comes into our mind, acknowledge it, and then change it. Put in the thought of the most peaceful place we know of, the most beautiful place we can imagine.

Or, if action is required, then draw forth the most positive action to our mind that we can and see a positive reaction coming from it. If we do not get the reaction we are looking for, do it again. Keep a positive spin on the situation and eventually the situation will change.

Whether it is justified or unjustified, we have put ourselves in that situation on purpose. The question of why we put ourselves there must be analyzed. We do it, not to beat ourselves with a stick, but to find the direction where our heart knows that we are supposed to go.

Setting ourselves up for failure is nothing more than an unconscious effort to change our direction. See it as such and decide that we are going to find our way to where we are supposed to be.

Tigger or Eeyore?

We have the power to control our world in a positive and peaceful way. Take control of our thoughts and we gain control of our world.

Let's use another example of thoughts. One that strikes close to home for many of us. Bills. People tend to concentrate on the money they owe and the bills they have to pay. When a bill arrives, it should be about a three minute process. We receive the bill, look at it, and either write a check or decisively decide when we can pay it, and deal with it at that specific time. Then, we are done with it for today.

Spending more than three minutes on the bill focuses our energy on what we don't have instead of what we do have. When we change our focus from the bill to the way to generate greater finances, then we end up getting fewer bills and greater finances.

This does not mean that we ignore the bill, as that is a negative thought. We create a positive thought about when we are going to pay that bill, and how we are going to generate more money than the bill is for, and end up ahead. Clean water.

If we slip from the now and the bill comes to mind, be aware of our thoughts, and decide when and where that bill will be handled, in a positive way, and move on. We have made the decision so there is no more need to think about it. Move on.

Change our thoughts from what we don't have to what we are receiving. Change our thought to money flowing to us. Yes, we have to do something to create that flow, but with the right mindset, it happens. Start with "money comes to me easily." Keep that thought foremost and soon enough we find that we are creating ways to fulfill our expectations.

Freedom to…not freedom from.

Manifestation

Thought is energy. Energy is either positive or it is negative. There is no neutral energy. Energy attracts like kind energy. This is a scientific fact.

We are practicing being aware of our thoughts every moment. Before we know it, we have replaced the negative thoughts with positive thoughts. With positive thoughts come possibilities. With possibilities comes luck.

Remember one of the definitions of luck…when preparation meets opportunity. Positive thought allows us to be prepared and recognize opportunity. Put our mind on preparation. When the opportunity arises we will not only recognize it, we will be ready to take advantage of it. We will be in the position to "get lucky."

Action Steps for the Week

- Become aware of our thoughts and how they make us feel. Find the positive in a negative. Find the forgiveness in sin. Find the good in bad. Find the Invisible Truth, the real truth, in lies.

- Decide on the best outcome for the thoughts we have regarding a current circumstance. Remember that positive and how it makes us feel. See the outcome.

- Recall a happy moment. Feel it. Feel our exuberance. Look at the main object or person in front of us in the memory. Smile. Do this every morning.

- When we find ourselves with a negative thought coming into our mind, be aware of it and make it into a positive. Turn what we don't or can't do into something that we are happy to do or choose to do. (Instead of "I don't want to walk in the rain," practice using "I choose to sing in the rain.")

Law and Principle # 3

The Spoken Word

Speech is the mirror of the soul; as a man speaks, so he is.
— Publilius Syrus

There is power in the words each of us speaks. If we put our hands to our throats and speak, we feel a vibration. That vibration attracts other vibrations of the same magnitude.

Positive speech attracts positive vibrations. Negative words attract negative vibrations. Therefore, it is essential that we be aware of the things that come out of our mouths. What we speak is a function of our thoughts, of our consciousness. We are manifesting our thoughts by speaking them, through reinforcement. In other words, if we say something, we have a tendency to believe it. Every single word we speak, every single word...carries power. The power of these words is usually greatly underestimated.

Most of us are so unaware of the power of our words that we are not even conscious of the effect we are creating with them.

The Effect of the Spoken Word

A Japanese researcher and author, Dr. Masaru Emoto, found that the molecular structure of water could be changed through the spoken word. The change is based on the vibrational magnitude of the energy (words) being directed around it. The actual structure of the water turned into a beautiful thing when it was surrounded by positive speech, and changed to a very ugly, distorted structure when surrounded by negative speech. To learn more about this, google the doctor's name and this study will come up.

This follows a law of science; the result of positive speech is the water transforms into a lovely structure. There is nothing "woo-woo" nor "New Age" about it. Look at the empirical proof.

Under a microscope, the molecular structure of the water subjected to good vibrations looked much like the beauty of snowflakes, the essence of purity. It is the beauty of nature at its finest. The structure of the water that had been subjected to negative vibrations from "ugly" words was fractured, dark and ugly. It was actually a startling result!

Our bodies are made up of approximately 70 percent water. Water is our lifeline and the quality of our lives is directly connected to the quality of our water. The use of negative thoughts and words, phrases or terminology, by definition, creates ugly, distorted molecular structures within the water that makes up our bodies. It is apparent that the words I speak, due to the effect they have on the molecular structure of the water that makes up my body, have good or ill effects on my health, and the health of those around me.

Thus, it is essential that we are aware of the things that come out of our mouths. The words I speak are a manifestation of the thoughts I have. However, as I become conscious of the words I speak, I change the thoughts I have. In so doing, I begin to fill my bucket with clean water, thereby ridding the bucket with all of the murky water I have blasted into it.

Most people are aware of the old saying "If you can't say something nice about someone, then don't say anything at all" or a slight variation thereof. This isn't just the right thing to do; there are scientific reasons for this. When we are talking negatively about someone or something, negative vibrations attract that negative into our life. Logic dictates that the opposite is also true; positive information spoken about someone or something attracts positive into our lives.

If there is nothing good to say, say nothing and keep the attraction neutral, at least through our words. Remember, there is no such thing as a neutral attraction, at least in our outward response, which brings it back to thought. If the thought is negative, it attracts a negative. I have not voiced my opinion, so I have not reinforced my thought through speech. It is now up to me to clear up my thoughts on the matter.

How can I change that negative thought, whether deserved or not, to a positive one that allows me to work through the situation in a way that creates the best outcome?

A positive thought has as infectious of an outcome as a positive word, within me.... Within me.

As I think about the people who are in my life, both personally and professionally, I think of them in their positive attributes. Thus, I understand how best to approach them in order to receive from them the results I desire. There is something good about everyone. It is my goal to keep focused on the positive; I am finding that good. (Yes, I know, sometimes that is a stretch...which, in itself, is a negative thought I am working on.)

In every association, we are taking and we are giving. Are we, or they, taking more than giving? This may sound like manipulation, and in essence, it is.

Manipulating a person for my best interest should be in their best interest also. That is the way it is. This is not to be confused with Machiavellianism. Quite to the contrary, this positive life strategy is not to be performed "at any cost." It is to be performed as "our combined efforts being what is best for us both and for the world around us."

Truthfully review each of our associations. Does each person receive something desired, relished or cherished from each union?

Another old adage..."Make the best of a bad situation." There are reasons these old adages survive through time. Often, the thought we have is what we don't desire to have happen. Simply change it to what we do desire to have happen. Oftentimes all we have to do is to change the conversation, or the thought, from what is wrong to what is right. Remember, when we indicate what is wrong, the finger of fault is often pointed directly at ourselves. What we are thinking or saying about another is what we really think about ourselves.

I remember a story, from years ago, that a friend of mine told me. He was a football player who told of how he was in a game and his particular defender was getting the best of him the entire game. Not only that, but his opponent was taunting him at every opportunity. This was really getting to my friend, and as he described it, his entire focus was on how he could "get this guy." At half-time the coach, who had seen the battle my friend was having on the field, gave a speech about focusing on our own performance and bettering ourselves with each "play" in life, and taking our focus off how we can best our opponent. Something resonated with my friend.

On the first play from scrimmage in the second half, my friend got the ball. He didn't make many yards on his run, and he was hit thunderously by his opponent. When his opponent got up and started taunting my friend again, all my friend did was yell at the guy, "Great hit!" and he slapped his opponent on the backside. The opponent's tone immediately changed. They were no longer enemies; they were combatants in a game. They had fun playing, and it took my friend's focus off of how to best his rival and put it back onto how he could perform better. This allowed him to suddenly see something he hadn't noticed before. He took advantage of the fault he spotted in the other team's formation and ended up scoring the winning touchdown. After the game, the two had quite a conversation. They became good friends.

My friend took the focus off of the personal battle and put it back on the game.

Where is our focus?

Look around us. Focus on our favorite "game" in our lives. Contemplate it until we can spot a factor to improve.

Think about applying that concept for a minute. When we hear someone (or ourselves, for that matter) gossiping negatively about another, what the gossiper is actually expressing is their dissatisfaction with a negative in their own lives. While they are talking, their finger is pointing squarely at their own nose. Can we help them with that?

We are masters of the unsaid words, but slaves of those we let slip out. — Winston Churchill

Think about the people with whom we communicate on a daily basis. Think of the ones we enjoy talking with. They are usually the energized ones who are full of possibilities, ready to take a situation and make it better. These are the people who we are most attracted to. These are the people who are kind and gentle and full of energy. We are just naturally attracted to them.

If we are attracted to hopeful (positive) people, what characteristic of theirs would we like to emulate?

How many conversations have we all had that were circular and negatively patterned about someone or something? Nothing good is going to come of it. Someone is going to get hurt or destroyed through such talk, and many times it will be all parties involved in the conversation. However, it is okay to correct the record through straight talk that deals with the issue without destroying a person. When setting the record straight, it is critical that we reconstruct (fix) the issue being spoken about, and not attempt to denigrate the person speaking.

The positive ideology with which one speaks is a reflection of their view of the world. Conversely, the negative with which one speaks of another is a reflection of the negative that person feels about themself. When a person is negative about another it is because their bucket has murky water in it that resembles the mud of the one they are insulting. They find an attraction to that negative and, therefore, speak to others in terms that they themself understand. Those who initiate the majority of the negative gossip have the most character flaws themselves. Conversely, those who speak well of others are usually the most secure in themselves and their buckets are far cleaner.

Like attracts like.

Check out how clean the water is in the buckets of our friends. How does it look? If their bucket is filled with mud, why would we choose to keep that person in our life?

How many people do we know who have constant drama in their lives? How many who have relatively little? Or none? There is a constant in each of their lives. It is their speech and how they talk about other people and other things. Those who talk down or demean other people and things tend to have a great deal of drama in their lives, whereas those who restrain from speaking ill of others, or who express no opinion (adverse or otherwise), tend to have very little drama in their lives.

We let people know who we are through our character. Have good character. Let our character speak for us.

Structuring How We Speak

Some who are reading this right now are questioning this concept. The attitude is "I don't speak ill about people and I don't gossip...so why do I still have negative issues in my life?"

It is important to look at how we structure our language, and how we verbalize our thoughts. By changing how we speak, we change the way we think. This is a subtle, yet very important principle. It is based on the actual words that we use. Some of the words we currently use are so engrained into our patterns that we are not even aware of their connotations.

For example, if I state, "I want a new car" the word *want* is a word of lack. Lack is a word for not having. It is a word of incompletion.

If we choose to have lack, or not have, or have incompletion in our lives, we will continue to use the word *want*.

Words vibrate. We will continue to attract into our lives that which vibrates at the same level. Words are the materials that build the components of our outer and inner worlds. If we use the word *want* in our consciousness, our inner and outer worlds will be built on lack, or not having, and incompletion.

This is easy enough to correct at face value, but it is important to keep correcting it until a new habit or pattern is formed.

Using the example of the car, change our word structure. Instead of saying, "I want a new car," change it to "I *choose that* new car," or "I *will have that* new car." These are words of power. Even if it isn't time to purchase that particular car at this moment, we have set our sights on something specific that we have chosen, and the process of manifestation has begun.

When we use words such as *choose, have, capable*...we are using words of power. Words such as *want* are for those who have *chosen* to lack. It is a word of weakness. We will eliminate the word *want* from our vocabulary.

Another word that must be eliminated from our vocabulary is the word *try*. Either we do or we don't. To *try* is a deception. It is a deception to one's self by those who use it, and it is a deception to those towards whom the word is used. Someone who says that they are going to *try* is saying that they are going to fail.

Need is another word with a very legitimate meaning, yet is often used in an improper context. We all *need* air, water and food. We all *need* shelter from the elements. Beyond that, I cannot think of any place where there is a use for the word *need*, and therefore it is used inappropriately most of the time. It is used in forms that relay a context, and that is fine. I say, "I need to get to this meeting," as it would be awkward to say that "my attendance at this meeting is required and I must get moving in order to be there on time."

For the most part, it is a word that is to be avoided. In practice, it is a good thing to eliminate the word altogether, thereby creating the practice of speech necessary in the process of manifestation. "I am going to a meeting now. We will talk later." In this instance, I have created two positives. I am performing a valuable job, and we will talk later. Understand this, by saying that I will talk to a person, I have made a commitment. In order to continue in a positive fashion, it is necessary for me to talk to that person at some point about whatever it was that was of consequence at the moment.

When we become aware and conscious of the words coming from our mouths, we become aware that some of these words are setting us up for failure. When we see that, the words become easier to change. At first it is funny as we catch ourselves and correct ourselves, aloud, a lot. Just keep practicing. I say them too. The difference is that I am now aware when these words leave my mouth, and immediately correct them. (Right there I wrote *try* to correct them. I saw what I wrote, backed it up with the delete key and then said what I actually meant.) Remember, none of us are masters; we are all students.

Then, there are the waffle words. Maybe. Perhaps. The partial phrase, I think…as in I think I can do that. These words and phrases leave us open for failure. Far more powerful are phrases like "yes, I can" or "yes, I will" or "yes, I will learn that."

There are many times in our lives when no is the right answer. It is important to know how and when to say no. There is strength in it which is far superior to that dishonorable, instantly regretted yes that comes out of our mouth occasionally. We know the one I am talking about. It is the one that creates no honor because of our resistance to doing whatever it is that we have agreed to do, followed by our inevitable failure to keep our promise.

We honor our word.

When we fill our lives with words that waffle, our lives (buckets) will overflow on either side of the waffle. Since a waffle word is an unsure word, it vibrates at lower levels and brings back to us lower level returns, negative returns. No more *maybe, might, perhaps* or *I think.* Eliminate them. (No, don't tell ourselves that we will try to.) When failure does occur, as it sometimes will, we acknowledge it, rephrase our energy, and move on.

Think twice before you speak, because your words and influence will plant the seed of either success or failure in the mind of another. — Napoleon Hill

We are putting ourselves in a position of power by speaking words of strength. I can. I will. I have. I am…or even, no.

The actual, physical power of the words we use cannot be underestimated. The vibration we put into the world is clear in a very physical way, as has been shown with water by Dr. Emoto.

Examples of How We Communicate

Wouldn't it be great if we knew everything about this course after one reading? Isn't it nice that we do have the opportunity to read these lessons over and over?

Do we see anything wrong with the above questions? Look at them again before going on. See if we can determine which of these words are deceptions.

Here is a clue. Wouldn't means *would it not.* Isn't means *is it not.* Phrasing these questions again with the meanings of the words, we come up with this: Would it not be great if we knew everything about this course after one reading? Is it not nice that we do have the opportunity to read these lessons over and over?

The implied negatives within these questions correspond to not understanding, not comprehending. Rephrase these questions into positive statements. It is great that we understand these teachings after only one reading. It is nice that we have the opportunity to read these lessons over and over again.

Change questions to statements. Make the statements affirmations. When I do this, I am on the path to manifestation.

We have been trained since birth to speak the way we do. It is now time to become aware of the things that come out of our mouths. When we become aware and conscious of the words we say, and how we say them, we begin to change the thought processes we use to form our ideas and how our consciousness perceives the world. It is then that we begin to restructure our language, our words, to create a positive vibration, thereby attracting more positive into our worlds.

We will be very clear and exact when we speak. When we speak with clarity, exactness and purpose, the things we choose to make happen in our lives will manifest more swiftly.

Saying "I choose a new car" is a fine statement, however, it is not clear. We will end up with a new car that is not what we really desired. "I am going to find and purchase a Volvo station wagon that is less than five years old with fewer than sixty thousand miles, that passes my mechanic's test, has leather seats, has a CD player, and costs less than twenty thousand dollars." This is a specific statement. Making this statement will manifest our reality.

Picture our choice. Give it specific words.

Two things are to be made clear. One is that it is essential that we make statements that are possible. The second is that we realize that there are limitless possibilities. Picturing that I am going to be a millionaire sitting on my big yacht is not enough. Everything is possible. It requires work…and we will discuss the value of work further into the book.

When we fill our buckets with words that are not clear and exact, then our buckets overflow with things that are not clear and exact.

Hope

The trickiest word in the languages of man is the word hope. It has been viewed by some thinkers throughout history as the incantation of evil. It has been viewed by others as the first, and last, bastion of faith.

To hope for something as a singular action is to create a negative energy that leads to pessimism, despair, defeatism, depression and isolation.

However, to hope for a desired outcome, to have faith in that outcome, means taking action to manifest that outcome. In this case, hope is a word of belief and faith. When hope is followed by action to realize the potential probabilities of the desired outcome, then hope itself becomes an action.

Hope, *as* a lone action, is negative energy.

Hope, *with* action, is positive energy.

To do nothing but hope is a fool's errand. To work toward our hope is the champion's way.

If all we do is hope, we'll get nothing. Keep hoping...but get to work.

The Power of Spoken Words

Positive words are essential. Directing how we actually think our positive thoughts is also essential. There have been numerous books, studies, etc., regarding the power of positive thought. Let's take that power of positive thought one step further.

A financial example.

I have made paying off my debt my number one goal. I decide that I am going to pay everything off within six months. I have this one particular bill that I am going to pay off this month, another which will be paid off within two months, two more within three months, and the rest within six months. I have a plan. I have the means and I will sacrifice to make this plan happen. Positive thinking, right?

What happens when something unexpected comes up that creates another bill? I have sacrificed in order to fulfill a plan that is now going to require adjustment or more sacrifice to complete. There is great potential to set myself up for failure.

The point is this. I have spent whatever amount of time creating a plan, filling my bucket up with how I am going to pay off my bills. The vibrations of my thoughts and words have focused only on bill paying, thus have created more bills. I am living in the future instead of living in the NOW. I am thinking and speaking of paying my bills, and the predictable conclusion is that I will receive more bills to pay. I created it.

In short, living in the now means creating a plan (budget) and then getting on with the living (now) part. Choose to create more abundance. See our positive cash flow as being greater than our expenses. Freedom to create abundance, not freedom from our bills.

The second point here is that we all have bills. We always will have bills. We will always be paying bills. (These sentences are spoken quickly and lightly, with the pride of responsibility, not with the apathy of despair.) The focus is to be changed from the bills to the creation of capital, the creation of money.

If I come up short in a month, I don't avoid the person or company to whom I owe a payment; I contact them before they can contact me. I give them my realistic intent, tell the truth, and then move on. I have created a positive energy by my actions.

I live within my means with my full intent of expanding my means. I expand my means through my thoughts and my words. I have begun manifesting my desired outcome.

Fully understanding this concept requires awareness, insight and practice. Our view of manifestation becomes clearer as we proceed with these lessons. Restructuring the way we speak goes a long way in changing the way we think to get our desired and positive results.

Psalms 23:1 The Lord is my Shepherd, I shall not be in want. (NIV)

As we are gaining a better understanding of how the universe and the laws of nature work, it becomes clearer why we shall not want. Again, *want* is a word of lack, not having and incompletion. The word *want* brings to us, very energetically, lack, not having and incompletion in our lives.

With the Lord as my shepherd I do not lack. With the Lord as my shepherd, I have all I choose, in abundance.

It is fascinating that many of the scientifically proven laws of the universe and nature were written into the scripture of the various religious and philosophical teachings that date back hundreds and thousands of years.

Invisible Truth, while showing how the laws of nature and the universe interact, uses many teachings from the bible. The teachings of the different philosophies and religions of the world all can be found to reflect many of the same things with regards to the power of the human mind and the laws of manifestation.

The writing of Invisible Truth came from the divine spark of the bible. We acknowledge our divine spark, whatever it may be, and fully honor it. We do our own research. Study, learn and thrive. Allow us to come together energetically in a place of connection in the universe that comes from love, peace and truth. We use biblical scripture as an example of truth that was written thousands of years ago, which science is just now starting to catch up with.

James 3:2-5 We all stumble in many ways. If anyone is never at fault in what he says, he is a perfect man, able to keep his whole body in check. When we put bits into the mouths of horses to make them obey us, we can turn the whole animal.

Or take ships as an example. Although they are so large and are driven by strong winds, they are steered by a very small rudder wherever the pilot wants to go. Likewise the tongue is a small part of the body, but it makes great boasts. Consider what a great forest is set on fire by a small spark. (NIV)

The spoken word is a powerful thing. A man who does not offend in his spoken word is considered to be a perfect man, and able to bridle his whole body. The power of our tongue is compared to the very small bit in a horse's mouth, which, in turn, controls the body of the horse. Our tongue is also like the rudder of a very large and powerful ship. Even when fighting fierce winds, that small rudder still controls the direction of that ship. The smallest of sparks can create the largest of forest fires. The spoken word is a very powerful thing.

Speak softly and powerfully.

It has been shown that we can change the molecular structure of water with the words that we speak. Again, our body is made up of about 70 percent water. The earth is made up of about 70 percent water. When we change 70 percent of the molecular structure of something, that something will be charged with either positive or negative energy.

That is power.

What would happen in the world if we all, all of humanity, all at once, said something positive? All of that positive energy would be released at the same time into the conscious world, and the energy would be incredible. When we speak, energy moves, and the movement of positive, high vibrating energy is a miraculous thing.

We can change the world with our tongues. War can turn to peace, starvation to nourishment, poorness to riches, sickness to health, and sadness to happiness.

It is time to raise our consciousness, and the consciousness of others. When we speak, we manifest physical realities into our lives. When we speak, we manifest and attract the same vibrational magnitude into the world around us.

Because we have this knowledge, we are responsible for creating positive energy.

Job 22:28 What you decide on will be done, and light will shine on your ways. (NIV)

In the King James version of the bible, the word decide is described as decree. Decree means a formal or authoritarian order, one having the force of law. Speak with positive authority and let the light shine upon our ways.

Matthew 12:36 But I tell you that men will have to give account on the day of judgment for every careless word they have spoken. (NIV)

What if it is me who has to account...to myself first on the day of reckoning?

Would I be happy watching a movie of my life? Would it be a comedy, a drama or a horror flick?

Think. How does it sound when we are speaking (thinking)? Is it positive or negative?

This does not mean we all become cheerleaders. We must acknowledge what our condition or situation is at any given time. It is what we think, what we say and what we do in any given circumstance that determines the outcome of the situation.

Because I love old sayings, here is another one. "Life is 10 percent of what happens around me and 90 percent how I react to it." There are things that are out of our control. How we react to these things is in our direct control.

Acknowledge the situation for what it is. Put into words the best thing that can be made of a circumstance. This goes a long way toward making the "best of a bad thing."

Restructuring Our Language

Instead of "I choose to lose some weight," use "I choose to be thin," or "I am thin."

Instead of "I choose not to be broke," or "I choose to pay my bills," use "money comes effortlessly. I am wealthy. I have abundance."

Instead of "I choose to no longer be sick," use "I choose health, energy and vitality."

If we take the negative words out of our vocabulary and restructure our words into the positive and the reaffirming, what we desire to happen manifests itself in a much more expedient way.

Again, at first, only at first, this is a difficult concept, but a very important one. Choice is just the first step. Now it is what we choose that is to be defined.

Choosing not to be sick, broke or fat keeps the focus on being sick, broke or fat. Choosing to be healthy, wealthy and thin creates exactly that. It brings the vibrational energy to the point of our focus.

We will keep our focus on the desired result, because when we keep it on the negative, we are drawn to that energy and it will keep manifesting itself. Keep the positive focus.

Here are two personal examples. When I was young, literally a starving college student, I remember saying aloud that I didn't care if I ever made any money, as long as I had cash flow and could afford to eat. Well, it took more than 30 years to break that thought process. Around the same time of my life, my back was sore and I said out loud that I had a bad back. Several back surgeries later, I can trace my back problems back to a single utterance made by one who knew no better. I know better now. I have no excuses. I create and manifest that which I choose.

As the old saying goes…"be careful what you wish for…." In this case it is better stated, "be careful of the things you say."

Our words are very creative and meaningful. They have a very powerful vibration. They attract to us that which we speak.

Our subconscious is very exact and precise. It does nothing but create our outer and inner worlds with the materials that we give it. Speak with the exact and precise words that we wish to create with. Use words of power. Words are a very large part of the materials that the subconscious uses. We now choose our words carefully, and with wisdom.

Every time we speak, we must be aware and conscious that the words we use are those that we wish to fill our buckets (our lives) with. Our words that we say right now are those that we are creating our future with. When we do the present moment correctly, the future will happen in a positive way.

Proverbs 21:23 He who guards his mouth and his tongue keeps himself from calamity. (NIV)

Proverbs 23:15-16 My son, if your heart is wise, then my heart will be glad; my inmost being will rejoice when your lips speak what is right. (NIV)

Restructure our language to the positive and we will keep our soul from troubles and our heart will rejoice.

Action Steps for the Week

- Review and practice the activities of *Bucket, Living in the Now* and *Thoughts*. (If necessary, go back and review them again.)

- Become aware and conscious of the words we speak and how we arrange those words. Actually hear what is coming out of our mouth. How does it sound to us?

- Become aware of the words in our thought patterns for the same reasons.

- Change our words and sentences to fit our positive desires, leaving out the negative words. It takes practice and thought. Have fun with it. Stumble, laugh, and correct our own words.

- Think about the judgments we are having with regards to what we are reading. Why are we coming to these judgments, with emotions wrapped around them, regarding what we are reading? We are now on our way to the process of self-awareness.

- Be aware of the things people say to us and how they structure their use of words. We are now beginning to hear patterns. Some are positive and uplifting. Some we recognize as negative and self-defeating. Awareness will retrain our subconscious faster.

- Remember, we are creating new habits. True change takes effort and time. I will be working on this for the rest of my life. Read these pages as many times as it takes in order to memorize them. When we desire a refresher, just pick the book up again and read whichever law and principle is most affecting us at the moment.

Law and Principle # 4

Belief and Faith

We are all prophets. Whatever we are speaking, we are creating.
— Christina Wollebek-Smith

We are living the "now"…now. We have become aware of our thoughts and how they affect our lives. We have become mindful of the words we use, the implications of those words, and their effect on our thoughts. We are beginning to understand the flow of energy and how we control it in a directed, organized way.

It is now time to believe. It is time to believe and have faith. It is time to believe in ourselves, in God, and in our lives.

Genesis 15:6 Abram believed the Lord, and he credited to him as righteousness. (NIV)

To believe in God is to believe in ourselves. To believe in ourselves is to believe in God. Said another way, to believe in God, I must believe in myself. God is in me.

Men often become what they believe themselves to be. If I believe I cannot do something, it makes me incapable of doing it. But when I believe I can, then I acquire the ability to do it even if I didn't have it in the beginning. — Mahatma Gandhi

Belief and Manifestation

Manifestation without belief is elusive, if not impossible. Many things are easy to believe; others are not. Some believe only after concrete, tangible evidence is presented. Others work on faith.

Some have similar beliefs. Some completely opposite. Some have beliefs that have been given to them. Some have beliefs that are directly against what they have been told or taught. Some base their beliefs on their life experiences. Some base their beliefs on their studies. Some believe very little, if anything at all, which is, in itself, a belief. Some believe everything they are told. Most of us are floundering somewhere in the middle.

Belief, often called faith, is the positive "knowing" that something exists, even without empirical evidence. Empirical evidence is, as defined, based on or characterized by, observation and experiment, instead of theory. Philosophically, empirical evidence is derived as knowledge from experience. Specifically, it is gleaned from sensory observation, and assumed from application of logic.

It is important to understand the definitions here, so we will take this a few steps further. Faith is defined as the belief in, devotion to, or trust in somebody or something, especially without logical proof. Most people would typically describe faith as having to do with God, and, by definition, that is true. However, faith can encompass, or not, many aspects of our life not related to our belief in God.

Belief: the acceptance of the truth of something; that something is true or real, often underpinned by the emotional or spiritual sense of certainty.

Though not exactly the same, the words faith and belief share enough common characteristics as to be interchangeable in these teachings.

Belief and Faith are extraordinary. With faith, nothing is impossible to us.

When we attach belief into the nine laws and principles of Invisible Truth, we create a powerful manifestation within our life that will be impossible to deny. Some may consider such manifestations to be miracles.

The initial "leap of faith" is the hardest part to creating abundance.

Live your beliefs and you can turn the world around.
— Henry David Thoreau

Getting There

Many of our beliefs come from, and are developed by, our life experiences. From the time we are born until this very moment, we are developing our beliefs. Each belief is seeded deep in our subconscious mind. It is made up from our experiences, emotions around those experiences, and the memories of the consequences of those experiences. Our conscious mind gives credence and weighs the intangibles of these experiences, and then judges them as good or bad. The light switch is either on or it is off.

The switch being on or off at a particular juncture of our thought (neural) process determines where the thought will lead to. Our neural pathway may take any particular thought through thousands, if not millions, of junctures instantly, while processing what is about to come out of our mouths. Our logic processing is infinitely more rapid than that of a computer. The miniscule difference between us (bundles of conscious energy) and the artificial intelligence that is here, and will be coming in the very near future, is the emotional filters we put our process through.

The difference between our processing and that of a machine is that we have emotion.

To make it a little more comprehensive, let's go back to the bucket analogy. Our conscious minds are made up of the things we think, the words we say, the things we work towards, etc. In other words, this is the hose that we fill our subconscious minds (our buckets) up with.

Our subconscious minds do nothing but create with the materials we have filled our buckets with. It also wraps a judgment and an emotion around each and every experience in our lives, which gives us the pathways on which a future, seemingly related stimulus is judged, rightly or wrongly.

Our bucket of life begins to overflow with the experiences…and moves our minds with the emotions and memories. Remember, what flows out of our buckets is what we are conscious of. Based on our memories and the emotion attached to those memories, we created a belief. Beliefs affect everything we do, see and experience. Memories and judgments, the cause and effects of our lives, are what we fill our buckets with. This forms how we see the world. Most of our judgments were formed when we were young…when we were not so much on autopilot. Our subconscious mind is generally fully developed by about the age of six. After that we run on autopilot about 99 percent of the time.

Some of the things we think we believe have been handed to us. Our parents took us to church and told us to believe in God. They didn't tell us why; they just told us this was the way. Some of the things we think we believe were taught to us in school. We were told that "this is the way it is," or was, and we never questioned it. We think we believe much of what we were taught is truth. Some of the things we believe through repetitive experience; we have categorized them as a given when, indeed, they may not be.

Ever asked someone why they believed what they believed and the answer was "I don't know?"

Remember, we are part of a herd. In order for the herd to think, act and behave in ways that are best for the overall benefit of that herd, we are taught certain and specific things that will bring our mindset and belief systems in line with the herd mentality.

Wake up.

Do not believe in anything simply because you heard it. Do not believe in anything simply because it is spoken and rumored by many. Do not believe in anything simply because it is found written in your religious books. Do not believe in anything merely on the authority of your teachers and elders. Do not believe in traditions because they have been handed down for many generations. But after observation and analysis, when you find that anything agrees with reason and is conducive to the good and benefit of one and all, then accept it and live up to it.
— Buddha

Autopilot

We don't think about turning the doorknob to enter the other room, we just do it...autopilot. We don't think about tying our shoes, we just do it...autopilot. Unfortunately, we don't often think before we speak because, again, we are on autopilot. Virtually most of our functions we do in life are done on autopilot, which is as it should be...if the water in our bucket is crystal clear. However, the things we do on autopilot are giving our subconscious minds, usually through reinforcement, the materials that make up our inner and outer worlds. Becoming conscious of the subconscious is necessary in order to clear the path and scrub the bucket clean.

We will retain autopilot for the involuntary actions that simplify our life, such as our heartbeat, respirations and digestion. We are taking back control over all other (re)actions of our body, such as who makes our heart beat faster and how our body physically reacts to others.

Depending upon the reinforcements that have been received by the time we are about six, we have heard a lot of "no," "don't do that," "you can't," "we can't afford that,"...and this is common in every family. Then, there are the things that are said that can create a self-perception that is not consistent with the truth. "You can't do that." "That _____ is ugly." "That's too much for you." The list goes on and on. The adults who have come from that negative house are fighting an uphill battle from the beginning. If that is us, change it. Even if it wasn't us, change it anyway.

No youngster should know the word "hate," much less utilize it. For that matter, no one of any age should know the word "hate." It is such an ugly word. Just writing the word is bothering me. In reality, it is a word in our lexicon of verbiage that is used far too easily in today's society. Strike it from our vocabulary.

For those of us who are parents, we know the challenge. The huge challenge of finding the right balance of discipline and positive reinforcement is constant. It is a direct reflection of how we view ourselves. Some of what we dump on our kids was dumped on us as children. Breaking the cycle is an even larger challenge.

Today's Hope

Some people have naturally clean buckets. Some were just born smiling. Some middle and youngest children are relaxed and happy as they contently follow their older sibling's complex ideas or instructions; they're just as calm when they take over. Some are natural peacemakers in the family.

Some attributes seem innate. For some, tapping into the God consciousness or the Universe is a natural ability we are born with. For others, it is something we consciously practice on until our skill improves. Using the Invisible Truth to cleanse our bucket starts us on this pathway.

Some children, often called Crystal or Indigo Children, are more naturally able to tap into the God consciousness. With innate peace of mind (clean bucket), guileless intentions (clean thoughts and words), and unchallenged belief, this comes naturally to them.

Some people are so emotionally clean than they are true empaths.

Empathy: the intellectual identification with or vicarious experiencing of the feelings, thoughts or attitudes of another. This is more commonly known as actually sharing another person's emotions. These are people who do more than sympathize with our worries; they empathize. They feel our agony. They share in our joys. Perhaps their emotions are less entwined in their past baggage, thus more available for caring. These are good people to be around on the worst and the best days of our life.

Some people "feel it in their gut." Their instincts may be innate (genetic), environmentally developed, or both. They too are good people to be around on the essential days.

Some animals are predisposed to similar abilities. The dog who travels a hundred miles to return to his human knows where he feels at home. He defines home as the place of abundant giving and receiving, of thankfulness and forgiveness. And love.

Each of these is a useful ability to develop in ourselves and in our children.

I have a dream that my four little children will one day live in a nation where they will not be judged by the color of their skin but by the content of their character.
— Martin Luther King, Jr.

Become aware of being aware. Put our judgment away. Allow our minds to field all of the possibilities. Feel the instinct that wells up within us. Tap into the universal consciousness....

I am aware that there is more to the universe than that which I understand or can even ponder. Knowing that, I allow myself to tap into the knowledge of the universe by acknowledging its presence.

It is all energy. Go with the flow. Peace will follow.

Thought, Words and Belief

We have been taught to speak with words that are, by their definitions, limiting. Words such as: Want. Try. Can't. The self-limiting words we have been taught are in great abundance in our lives. While we have been on autopilot, our buckets have been filled with things that are now reflected in our outer selves, in our outer world. Our outlook on the world is based on what our bucket is filled with, and by the time we hit our teens, our outlook on the world is pretty much set in place…or, rather, it has been until today, until we recognize the Invisible Truth.

Somehow, without our paying much attention, adulthood comes along…and with it comes the questions.

- Why is my life like this?
- Why am I not further ahead?
- Why am I not happy?
- Why do the same bad things keep happening to me?
- Why am I angry all the time?
- What is the true meaning of life?

We all have questions. What are our top three?

Choice

Now for some good news. We can get ahead. We can be happy. We can change our lives, and the experiences in our lives…and it will change our beliefs.

All this requires is choice. It is up to us to CHOOSE.

It is time to get off autopilot. It is time for us to take control of our lives. It is time for us to be conscious of the Invisible Truth and choose the correct way.

Through these laws and principles we are learning to reprogram our subconscious minds to create our desired results. We are learning a step-by-step method to change the beliefs that we have created that hold us back. We are learning to rid ourselves of the destructive beliefs that create destructive behavior in our lives.

Neuropeptides

First, we learn the Invisible Truth. This book will explain, in depth, what happens to our bodies…and how experience, emotion and memories relate and connect to belief, and therefore, to faith.

Here is the tease…we have a biochemical pull towards things that we attract. We will learn how to use that biochemical pull to attract the positive into our lives. This step will be a key in making a positive and permanent change in our lives.

Specifically, that biochemical pull becomes an addiction. We have become addicted to how we process the material, emotional and physical stimuli in our lives.

The concept of neuropeptides is a tricky one to describe. We get a lot more technical in the later chapter, *Unveiling the Neural Mystery*. For now, we are going to give a general description we can immediately put to use.

A neuropeptide is a chemical influencer that speeds the reactive processing of the brain by lubricating the predisposed pathways through which a thought travels. It is a memory within the pathway at the cellular level that allows for the (re)action to occur at an expedited rate. In other words, we don't have to "reason through" each stimulus that comes to us. Neuropeptides produce several functions, two of which are the "speed influencer" and a "directional influencer."

The direction a thought will instantly travel is influenced by the "traffic cops" that have been installed in our brains and bodies, at a cellular level, through the experiences (energy) that have already been created in our lives.

In other words, neuropeptides dictate the speed and direction of the firing of neurons in the reactive process of our bodies to a specific external stimulus in a set path of previous results.

Okay, time to take that thought back a notch. To use a physical example, we know, at a cellular level, that if we stick our hand in the fire it is going to hurt. To use an emotional example, we know that if we have a screaming and yelling fight with our spouse, it is going to hurt. Could it be both a physical and emotional response that we have to chocolate?

How about those people who are, seemingly, always grumpy? Are they addicted to the way they act? As Shirley McLean's character said in *Steel Magnolias*, "I'm not crazy…I have just been a very bad mood for 40 years."

"This is just the way I am." Well, how's it working for you so far?

The processes that run our brains, for lack of a better term, are predisposed, through neuropeptides, to fire information through particular and specific pathways in order to quickly integrate the incoming information into the framework of our experiences and beliefs.

It's when we attempt to drive a round peg into a square hole that sends our brains into a frantic, confused overdrive. The transmitters and receptors of our brain (the areas where neuropeptides sit, waiting for a signal to go) begin to sizzle and the result is the inevitable rationalizations necessary to make what we are seeing fit with what we believe.

In other words, if every cell in my body is accustomed (programmed) to my being mean and ornery, due to a 40 year habit (addicted), and someone suddenly tells me to be nice, then I don't even have an immediate response for them, much less an instantly kind reaction.

Here are some simple examples to help us wrap our heads around our personal neuropeptides.

Our addiction to coffee is a physical one. "Every cell in my body" craves that first cup in the morning. Moreover, "I can't wake up fully without the caffeine." Addiction. We could choose to be fully awake and aware sans coffee.

The mere thought of chocolate fudge appears and the body responds. The mental and physical addiction is empowering an emotional response which increases the thought that "I must have that chocolate" tenfold.

We see someone we dislike or have wronged or are afraid of; our whole body sags backwards or shrinks downward to cower and hide. Our brains send out "bad person" neuropeptides and our bodies respond with our preprogrammed reaction. Hide.

We send out "good friend" neuropeptides and our bodies respond by gravitating forward. This increases our emotional excitement at seeing our friend, which multiplies our physical joyful response of enthusiasm.

Becoming aware of the visceral reactions to the stimuli within our lives is necessary. The energy we put into and around our instinct might be earned, but its validity must be examined, primarily around negative feelings. A good example...caller ID. When we see the IRS is on the phone, how does it make us feel? How about our phone ringing in the middle of the night? For that matter, our boss's boss just got off the elevator and is walking straight towards our office? How about the thought of having to do calculus? Driving to the store in a blizzard? When our significant other says, "We've got to talk"? When the doctor says, "Your test results are in...sit down"?

The point to Invisible Truth is that we can control these visceral reactions, when we choose to, through being aware of them and installing new habits that create new pathways through which stimuli travel.

What will happen if we cut off the supply to our body's "fear" neuropeptides? If we replace the "cower now" response with "I am calm," then our body's "get ready to hide" demands will die of hunger. Pretty soon, our body will stop requesting the hiding because it has learned that it will not get what it desires; it will learn that the only "food" it is now being fed is "I am calm."

Cower or calm. It is our choice.

Now it is time for us to realize that for all the energy that we have around specific pleasantries, we have as much, if not more, negative energy around other things that no longer serve us.

Think of it this way. Here is a visual example of a neural pathway so we can visualize how to change the path itself. I pull up to the house in my car every day and park in the same spot on the street. Instead of walking around to the driveway and in through the walkway there (my wife's car is always parked there, blocking the way, and there is no room in the garage because it is still packed with the stuff from our old house and some day we are going to have that garage sale…), I walk across the lawn every day for a year. I create a pathway through the lawn. My wife and I decide that enough is enough. Springtime comes and we decide to have the mother of all garage sales. Everything goes. We finish with a few dump runs, because even the garage sale buyers won't take the junk and garbage.

Clear at last.

My wife starts parking in the garage, and we start to park in the driveway and walk up the walkway into the house. The pathway in the grass starts to mend and grow new grass. The house is looking better. Every now and then, because we are so used to the old way of doing things, we automatically pull up to where we used to park on the street, turn off the car and start to get out. We look down at the old pathway and say to ourselves, "…oh yes…," start the car up and drive it into the driveway because we have consciously started a new way to do things.

That old pathway through the grass no longer serves us. This new pathway is much better.

Think about the most destructive pathway we have created in our life that is no longer useful and is not getting us the results we choose. Decide what we are going to do to create an extremely positive pathway (a mental garage sale?) today.

Think it. Speak it. Believe it.

Our new pathway creates our desired results and the grass on the old pathway eventually grows over so we wouldn't know that it had ever been there. Occasionally we will pull up to the old spot (our old way of thinking), recognize it for what it is, change over to the new spot and not ever retread over old ground.

Put the book down for a minute. Think about this one for a few minutes. What pathways were given to us that are no longer serving us? What pathways are we removing the enveloping emotion and judgment from? What pathways are we changing to new pathways to get to where we desire? Remember, the first step is seeing the pathway for what it is, and consciously deciding to change it.

What pathway in our life most represents this one huge example? What do we require to choose right now to change our parking spot to the driveway so the front lawn can heal? Make that decision. Change it.

The Power of Belief

Belief…and the power of belief, has been studied in scientific and controlled environments. Here is an example.

Effect of Belief on Psychic Phenomena: Performance in a Card Guessing Task. (By Kevin Walsh and Garret Moddel, University of Colorado, *Journal of Scientific Exploration*, volume 21, number 3, pages 501-510, 2007.)

The following is a synopsis of what was found and what is stated. It is the end result that we are concentrating on here.

The study looked to find out if belief had any role in the correct guessing of what symbols lay beneath a random pattern of cards. The control group was picked at random and were given a fact sheet that either supported psychic phenomena or a fact sheet that dismissed random phenomena. The subjects were divided into four groups.

One group was designated as previous believers (those who believed that the cards symbol could be correctly guessed) who received pro-psychic phenomena fact sheets.

One group was designated as previous believers who received anti-psychic phenomena fact sheets.

One group was designated as non-believers (those who did not believe that the symbols could be correctly guessed) who received pro-psychic phenomena fact sheets.

One group was designated as non-believers who were given anti-psychic fact sheets.

The experimenter controlled a stack of 100 zener cards. Zener cards were first used by the famous parapsychologist, J.B. Rhine, during his studies of extrasensory perception (ESP). The basic premise is that a minimum of 25 picks from each subject with a correct "guess" of more than 10 symbols shows significance in prediction.

After the random, controlled study was finished, the following results were published.

The previous believers with pro-psychic phenomena fact sheets scored the highest.

The previous believers with anti-psychic facts sheets scored second highest, the previous non-believers with pro-psychic fact sheets third, and the previous non-believers with anti-psychic fact sheets last.

The results show that the significance of belief carries a strong indication of the outcome of a controlled event where all of the variables are known. The variance in the results between those who believed and those who didn't was quite significant. The variance between the groups' results was huge, not miniscule.

Relating this study to our lives is easy. Most of us know all the variables within a certain parameter of each event, decision or action in our lives. Belief in the results strongly controls the outcome of our actions.

What did this prove? Belief can cause results to be as expected.

Cause and effect. The basis of the study of science. Belief, or faith, has been scientifically shown to create an effect.

In other words, when we know (believe) what the results are going to be of any particular action we take, those results are, baring outside random influence, going to be exactly what happens after any given action we take (we cause). "I believe that if I take this action, I will get these results." The three key words are belief, action, results.

That bears reiteration. Belief, action, results.

For those who believe, no proof is necessary. For those who don't believe, no proof is possible. — Stuart Chase

Another Study

Teachers Expectancies: Determinants of Pupil's IQ Gains. (*Psychological Reports*, Volume 19, pages 115-118. Robert Rosenthal, Harvard University, Lenore Jacobson, South San Francisco Unified School District.)

In a test given to young school children (primarily grades one and two), to predict academic blooming and intellectual gain, it was determined that expectations significantly impacted the outcome of a child's IQ gain.

The study was spread over eighteen classrooms. The hypothesis was that each teacher was given a random sample of children's names within their classrooms who were "tested" by the controllers as being significantly bright, thereby creating certain expectations within the teachers.

In fact, there were no tests and the children's names were randomly chosen. Over an eight month period of time, the "bright" students (approximately 20 percent of the students within the control group), showed a significantly greater IQ gain than the students who were not named to the teachers.

Understand this. It is quintessential. It was not just the students being tested; it was primarily the expectations of the teachers. The students were told that they were bright, raising their expectations as well as the actual expectations of the teachers. The expectations of the teachers were met, primarily because of their belief. This wasn't a test of the students; those results were easy to predict. This was a test of the beliefs of the teachers.

The teachers expected certain results. Those results were achieved, primarily through their expectations. This was the sole criteria implicated for the testing; it was the cause (Or was it the effect?) here. The results show the power of expectation (belief) to be a very powerful thing.

The Placebo Effect

One thing that most people are aware of is the power of the "Placebo Effect." The studies around this effect usually have had to do with psychological or health measurements through the power of belief.

A placebo, as used in research terms, is an inactive substance or procedure used as a control in an experiment. The placebo effect is the measurable, observable or felt improvement not attributable to an actual treatment.

The studies are so diverse and widespread that to quote any would mean to miss more profound ones. I will cut straight to the chase here.

If we believe something strongly enough, there is a very good chance that the result will be as we expect. The best doctors out there could feed us sugar pills. If he or she convinced us, without the shadow of a doubt, that these pills were just exactly the right cure for whatever ailed us, there is a good chance that it will cure us. What really happened was that our belief in our healing was pure.

Add in the factor that we chose to heal. We believed we could and should so we did. We chose to live.

Belief (faith) is extremely powerful.

Luke 8:50 Hearing this, Jesus said to Jairus, "Don't be afraid; just believe, and she will be healed." (NIV)

Expectation of Results

Whether it is our expectation of the results of our children or the expectations of the results in our own lives, what we believe is what we are going to get. As the old adage goes…"whatever you believe"…is right.

"Whatever you believe"…is what we are going to get in our lives.

Whatever the mind can conceive and believe,
the mind can achieve. — Napoleon Hill

What we expect and believe is going to happen in our own lives is a very powerful influence on the actual results of any action or reaction that occurs. Another old saying…"expect miracles." When we expect miracles, they occur. Sometimes not in the form we thought they would, but they occur, nonetheless.

This discussion begs the question: what constitutes a miracle? A miracle is described as an extraordinary event in the physical world that surpasses all known human or natural powers. It is considered to be some form of manifestation, ascribed to a supernatural power such as God.

The point is this. When we expect (believe) in our own lives, miracles happen. Desires and expectations are powerful determinants in manifesting the reality of our inner and outer worlds. Miracles happen. Science can deny that. Fine. There are physical explanations for everything. I accept that. Some physical explanations I choose to call miracles. I choose not to have to understand how they happen. I do choose, however, to believe in them, and that I can manifest them.

Miracles have been described as events that science cannot explain…yet.

When we view the interconnection of what we think, speak and work towards…and the experiences, emotions and memories that these thoughts and words develop in us…then add in the remaining laws and principals outlined in this teaching, belief is the result.

When interconnected energy that flows from expectations and belief is carried within the proper channels of the positive, then nothing is impossible to us.

…Then, nothing is impossible to us…miracles?

Belief, next to love, is the most powerful force of energy there is. If we doubt this, think about the negative energy there has been in the world throughout the ages and the destruction that it has created. A lot of that negative energy has been created "in the name of God." It is cliché, I know, but the forces of good (energy) have, for the most part, always triumphed over the forces of evil (negative energy). Belief (in the right way) is a force that will not be denied. When it is a force that can be denied, we will know that we have hit the end of times. I do not see that happening anytime soon, if ever. People are good. We have God in us. Let Him out.

Fear creates a particular negative emotion that emanates a lower level vibration. We attract things to us of the same vibrational magnitude. Think about those in our life whose glass is always "half empty." It always seems to be half empty and they struggle with everything in their existence. We aren't just talking money here. Everything is turmoil and struggle. We can see them right now, right?

Positive attracts positive, and negative attracts…well, we get it. When we believe, then we expect what we believe. There are many powerful factors in the concept of belief. The magnitude of our beliefs cannot be underestimated.

Matthew 9:29-30 Then he touched their eyes and said, "According to your faith will it be done to you"; and their sight was restored. (NIV)

Faith is Belief. According to our faith, will it be done to us. Because of these blind people's faith, they were healed. Remember, Jesus told us His lessons were in parables. What was Jesus saying here? What He said was "according to your faith," not "according to my faith."

Right after this verse, Jesus swore the healed to secrecy. This was because Jesus desired those who witnessed the healing to know it occurred due to the blind's faith, not because they were healed by someone else.

Matthew 9:20-22 Just then a woman who had been subject to bleeding for twelve years came up behind him and touched the edge of his cloak. She said to herself, "If I only touch his cloak, I will be healed." Jesus turned and saw her. "Take heart, daughter," he said, "your faith has healed you." And the woman was healed from that moment. (NIV)

I Believe. I Have Faith. What I believe in, have faith in, is up to me.

I believe I create the world in which I live, given any circumstance or any situation.

I believe in me.

The Parable of the Mustard Seed

Luke 17:6 He replied, "If you have faith as small as a mustard seed, you can say to this mulberry tree, 'Be uprooted and planted in the sea,' and it will obey you.

Matthew 17:20 He replied, "Because you have so little faith. I tell you the truth, if you have faith as small as a mustard seed, you can say to this mountain, 'Move from here to there' and it will move. Nothing will be impossible for you." (NIV)

Faith. Belief. Interchangeable. What was once unimaginable is not only possible, but now expected.

There is an old saying: "Faith can move mountains." It is time to Believe. What to believe is up to us. With the faith of a mustard seed, nothing is impossible.

It is time to get to work. Getting to work means studying these writings and taking notes. Creating new habits of thought. Take the things we learn and put them into action.

Believe. Take action. Create energy, and our belief increases.

Remember, this is a lifelong process. Be willing to do the work necessary to create actual change.

We now begin to see changes. We recognize miracles. In so many ways, when we combine belief with action, things begin to happen in our lives that we would never have previously expected. Our desired results may not immediately manifest themselves. The test is to keep reapplying the lessons of these teachings to the new set of circumstances and keep working, with faith, until the results we wish to obtain are realized.

Moving the Mountain to Find the Mustard Seed

Sometimes you have to move a mountain to find the mustard seed.
— Christina Wollebek-Smith

It is only a matter of time and belief. This is the test of true conviction. We must believe in ourselves first. Some of these changes do not happen overnight. However, we will see change fairly rapidly. Subtle, but the changes do begin immediately.

Remember, when we *try* to get good things, we come up short. When we *try*, when we *want*, we create lack. When we choose to believe, and work toward our beliefs, we create abundance.

The future is not a set of random things that just happen to us. The future is something we create, right here, right now.

Start. Now.

Changing a specific belief that is not serving us means breaking the neural connection associated around the particular emotions that created that belief. It is an actual physical change within our body. It is enough to know, right now, that belief is not something that just happens. For the most part, we were taught what to believe. It isn't necessarily ours, but was inherited from our parents or those in our young lives. Thinking that we believe is quite different than actually believing with strong conviction. Believing something comes from the very core of our physical body. The vessel that our soul is using at this moment has had a great influence on how our belief patterns have been created.

What we take into the next life is, to a certain extent, physically constructed by our bodies. What is our body telling us? How does our body tell us to think?

This is where science comes in. As we have discussed before, the way we judge the world is wrapped around the emotions associated to specific stimuli that have happened in our lives. The thought patterns around a certain stimulus have created a pathway through which any other similar stimuli run.

Our neural pathways are creatures of habit, so to speak.

A thought, or reaction, if you will, creates a biochemical surge which then creates a firing of neurons through the synapses of our brain. In that way, it creates a response pattern that has already been set up for any other thing that comes into our lives that looks the same (or similar). This is essential to our survival.

However, it also creates a method by which we deal with a new stimulus that may not serve us in the best way possible. It is for this reason that many self-help programs don't work. Our pathways of reaction around a certain stimulus are so engrained that no matter how many affirmations we say, our minds, subconsciously, aren't buying in.

Many of the pathways on which we react were built not consciously but through ignorance. We were young and not capable of the reasoning we have now. Our pathway was developed for us. To maintain a pathway that is destructive to our desired results is just as ignorant. To maintain doing things the same way, even though we know they don't work, isn't just ignorant; it is insane.

I once heard a definition of insanity as being "doing the same thing the same way, over and over again, somehow expecting a different result." "Doing something once that is painful, emotionally, mentally or physically, is a learning experience. Twice is a mistake. Third time is insanity."

Since the beginning of time, the reactions we have had were survival techniques. We either instinctively knew not to jump into the fire or we got a little too close when we were young and got burned. Once. Most of us have learned to harness fire as a tool to keep warm. A few of us have such a horrendous viral memory of fire from our childhood that we may freeze to death during a power outage in the dead of winter with three feet of snow outside.

Through the teachings of Invisible Truth, we learn how to change the "beaten path" of our thought and reaction process, in the areas we choose to change. In so doing, we unblock the areas in our belief systems that have been created by others, or by negative instances in our lives, so that we can become fully actualized in the understanding of what it is that we do believe.

Move the mountain. Find the faith. Find the mustard seed.

With faith, we heal.

Mark 9:23 "'If you can'?" said Jesus. "Everything is possible for him who believes." (NIV)

Action Steps for the Week

- I am becoming more aware and conscious of what it is that I think and speak. What I think and speak is what I fill my bucket with, the bucket that overflows to my life, creating experiences, emotions and memories which, in turn, develop my beliefs.

- I have begun the process of changing my inner beliefs by writing down affirmations and looking at them, thinking about them and verbally speaking them.

- I understand that these affirmations are not the end-all. They are the beginning. As I study further, I am examining the reasons why I believe certain things in my life. I am choosing to change the things that don't work for me. The things that were given to me by others aren't mine; I am choosing to change to a belief system that does work for me and brings to me that which I desire.

Remember: Today is a day that the Lord made. Be glad and rejoice in it.

These affirmations can be whatever it is that we choose. We are setting energy in motion to create ourselves with these affirmations. Use them. Continue to use them. Watch as goodness begins to blossom.

Here are some examples that we could all easily integrate into our beings.

I radiate love, happiness and joy.
I like, enjoy and choose laughter.
I exemplify wisdom.
Money is a "current of currency" flowing toward me.
I laugh. I laugh easily. I find humor in every innuendo.
I see smiles everywhere. I always enjoy smiling and nodding at passersby and seeing them smile back.
I feel gratitude spilling out of my heart.
I am lucky!

Law and Principle # 5

Work

*The big secret in life is that there is no big secret. Whatever your
goal, you can get there if you're willing to work.*
— Oprah Winfrey

As we have stated, the world is created of energy. It changes forms
throughout the universe through cause and effect. Each of us has
the ability to cause energy to change in ways that directly affect
our outer and inner worlds, our conscious and subconscious.

Energy, when utilized in a positive form, creates great benefits for
mankind, individually and collectively. As we create motion, we
create or change the direction of energy, both positive and
negative, which then attracts like energy, thereby creating a
spiraling or snowball effect. The more energy we generate, the
more we collect.

Positive energy can be multiplied in such a magnificent form that it
cannot be denied and it can achieve anything. Negative energy can
do the same thing to such an extent that the entire planet could
easily be destroyed were it not put into check by the balancing and
magnification of good energy (love).

Think about this. Think of examples throughout history. There are
plenty.

Think of examples in our lives. There are plenty.

Imagine a river rolling towards the sea. Along the way the river may run though a turbine, turning it, and thereby creating electricity. The electricity is captured and sent though a wire...to our house, so that we can turn on the blender for us to create our protein smoothie. This smoothie, in turn, will supply energy for our body in order for us to create our world, and thereby help create the world of the people and things around us.

It is all energy. We are energy. Energy flows from one form to another, never ending. The universe "begins and ends" with the flow of energy. We have the ability to harness immense energy for our favor. We all have access to infinite amounts of energy, in the form we choose. It is our choice whether that energy is going to yield positive or negative results in our lives.

It all starts with the energy of a thought. When we control the energy of that thought, making it into positive energy, we say positive words which, besides the positive effect those words have on the world around us, will reinforce the thought we had which began this redirection of energy. Through our reinforced positive thoughts and words, we create belief. With belief we begin the process of manifestation of the desired result in our lives. Now, it is time to create, and do, the work necessary in order for our beliefs to come to fruition.

Work requires discipline.

Discipline

Proverbs 13:18 He who ignores discipline comes to poverty and shame, but whoever heeds correction is honored. (NIV)

This can be a challenging word. Discipline.

Discipline requires work and work requires discipline.

I have purposely not emphasized this word until now. Had I focused on the word before now, I would have lost many readers.

The word is that intimidating. However, our lives require discipline. The changing of energy requires discipline.

Getting out of bed requires discipline. Eating breakfast requires discipline. Getting the children off to school requires discipline. Getting in the shower to get ready for work requires discipline. Getting into the car to go to work requires discipline…we get it.

We can handle that with exactitude. It's an easy life. Let's up the discipline. Happily getting out of bed requires discipline. Eating a healthy breakfast requires discipline. Getting the happy children off to school on time requires discipline. Getting in the shower, swiftly, to get ready for work, smiling, requires discipline. Getting into the car, on time, to go to work, cheerfully, requires discipline…we get it. Still not really asking very much out of ourselves, are we?

Changing our world, changing the world…changing the universe…requires discipline.

Discipline is the bridge between goals and accomplishment.
— Jim Rohn

We are changing our neural pathway about the connotations of discipline. We are learning to discipline ourselves in the way we think, speak and work. In so doing, it acts as a method through which we are learning to believe. Through belief, we create (manifest) great things. Through discipline, we are beginning to weave the nine laws and principles in the desired directions of our lives.

With self-discipline most anything is possible.
— Theodore Roosevelt

To manifest the things we desire, we must discipline our consciousness. We must discipline our consciousness in order to cleanse our bucket (our subconscious mind). We must cleanse our bucket in order to manifest greatness in our lives. Therefore, to get to where we desire to be, we must become disciplined in our approach to our lives.

We are becoming disciplined in the way we think, speak, act and react to all stimuli presented to us from both outside ourselves and within ourselves.

This in no way means that we are becoming automated drones of a particular thought process. Remember, each of us is an individual bundle of conscious energy. Each of us has our own unique set of life experiences through which our neural process works. Each of us is a different and unique soul.

This point cannot be underestimated nor taken lightly. Change requires discipline. Our lapse of discipline results in the dirty hose being slammed back into our buckets and being turned on full blast.

Discipline, with regards to the nine laws and principles of Invisible Truth simply means becoming aware...and remaining aware.

Becoming disciplined to remain aware of the things we think, the things we speak and the things we believe, when combined with these laws and principles, simply puts us on the path of creating the life we wish to create.

Become aware. Remain aware.

There are some excellent teachings that have been put into the world. As we have stated before, none of the information presented here is new. Whatever we have been taught, whatever we believe, it is a matter of discipline in adhering to those teachings. The heroes portrayed in our culture and throughout history have one thing in common...discipline. Their devotion to their beliefs spurred them to action in such a disciplined form that our admiration created their hero status.

Becoming and remaining disciplined to the creation of good in our lives is a lifelong exercise. At first it requires a great deal of work to create a new habit. As time goes on, the discipline we have created becomes second nature and there is no conscious work to it. The point being that a failure of results from any valid teaching is usually nothing more than a failure to remain disciplined. Whatever we are learning at the moment, we may revert back to our old way of doing things at the first sign of trouble. (Allow me to rephrase that, in the past, we used to automatically revert....)

Success requires that we become, and remain, disciplined in order to manifest the positive results in our lives.

In the teachings of Invisible Truth, we reiterate to you the principles that have been with mankind since the beginning of time. It is up to us to create the discipline to instill them into our conscious being, thereby cleansing our subconscious mind of the things that keep us from manifesting greatness.

Your vision will become clear only when you look into your heart.
Who looks outside, dreams. Who looks inside, awakens.
— CJ Jung

Our Work

Each of us works. We create. Some of us generate a great deal of currency through our creations. Some of us generate a great deal of joy in others when we create. Some of us work hard at not creating joy or money in our lives...but we are still creating. We are creating energy that, in turn, attracts like kind energy. When we work, we put energy into motion and the creation in our lives is quickened. It is imperative that we choose the work of good. It is imperative that we do good work.

Can anything be sadder than work left unfinished? Yes; work
never begun. — Christina Rossetti

The work of good comes from the energy of belief. When we believe...when we have faith in our work, our energy magnifies the power of our creation exponentially. The creation of positive energy then strengthens our belief, our faith, thereby creating an even more powerful being in that apropos snowball effect. Then, do it again. Believe, manifest, become more powerful.

Faith without work…is dead.

James 2:17 In the same way, faith by itself, if it is not accompanied by action, is dead. (NIV)

When we leave out work, we lessen and nullify the strength and power of the nine laws and principles. Work creates a smoother road to life. Work is a direct propellant to the manifestation of the desires we choose. We shall work towards whatever it is that we choose to manifest.

Because we choose better health, we are working with better health. Because we choose better finances, we are working with better finances. Because we choose a better relationship with whomever, we are working with a better relationship with that person.

Whatever we choose to manifest in our lives, we do so at a much faster pace when we combine belief and work.

There has been some misconception that if we think it and believe it, then it will happen or it will come. Remember, faith without action is not going to get us our desired results. This factor was exemplified in the movie, *Field of Dreams*, with different versions of the line (paraphrased): "If you build it, they will come." Work was required, not just mere thought. And it was rewarded.

Proverbs 15:19 The way of the sluggard is blocked with thorns, but the path of the upright is a highway. (NIV)

The path of the upright is the right one. The path of thorns is slow; the requisite battles involved don't get us to our desired goal. Much energy is expelled in the battles…"Can't you see how hard I'm trying?"…"Poor me, this is such a struggle, I work so hard…."

Take the highway. It is smoother, faster and easier. Far easier.

Proverbs 20:4 A sluggard does not plow in season; so at harvest time he looks but finds nothing. (NIV)

Who is the sluggard? What does that mean? The sluggard is the lazy person. It is the person who can come up with an excuse to not do anything they don't feel like doing. When the lazy people see the rewards of those around them, they will get jealous and begin to hate.

When it is cold and harsh out but the plowing must be done, we can make an excuse that it is too cold or we can take action by bundling up and getting to work.

Sometimes in doing our work, we require help. There is always a hand to reach out and help us. It is up to us to recognize the helping hand and grasp it. This isn't an excuse to let someone else do our work...it means that in some instances we require assistance.

One of the greatest things about mankind is our willingness to help. We must be ready and able to do the work, but sometimes we require "calling for backup." This might be through our church, social services, employer, counselors, friends, mentors, the educational system, family or whoever it may be.

When we have a clear, positive vision of where it is we are going and state it to the world, it is amazing how the energy of the world and the universe (God?) helps us realize our desire.

We all know the right thing to do.

We all instinctively know the work we must do in order to get to where we desire. Creating the excuses, the psychosomatic ills, and the walls around what we know must be done is the only starting point that leads to the task being "impossible." Granted, some desires require more work than others, and some desires are bordering the outside limits of reality, but nothing is impossible.

How many inspirational stories are out there? Hundreds? Thousands? I say the stories are limitless.

Look at the stories of the founding fathers of the United States. Just what in the world were they thinking? They made their minds up and manifested that which was their vision, their dream, if you will. It was a struggle, and a war was the result. The point was that enough people shared in the vision and that vision was not to be denied. It became a reality. Just for a moment, envision being one of the founding fathers.

Work while you have the light. You are responsible for the talent that has been entrusted to you. — Henri-Frédéric Amiel

Ninety-nine percent of the excuses out there are just that...excuses. They are not legitimate. They are the lazy people's way of saying they are not going to do something.

Reasons, on the other hand, may be legitimate. However, reasons can be dealt with. Reasons can be worked through in a pragmatic manner, actions can be taken to mitigate or neutralize them, and our course can continue toward our true destination. It will not continue on the same course we began, but the end result will be achieved, nonetheless.

This destination achievement is more feasible and requires less energy when the "reasons" are legitimate and are weighed down with as minimal amount of inappropriate baggage from our past as possible.

It is a matter of priority...and discipline.

It is also a matter of choice. We know what it is that we have to do, even if it isn't immediately evident. It is time to find the onramp to the highway and to get to where we are going, especially if we have lost our way. The hardest part is finding the onramp. Once we are on the highway, the road becomes a lot easier. Finding the onramp takes persistence, determination and practice.

Sometimes we can't even see where the highway is because the thorns are so daunting. If we keep hacking away at the thorns, and keep moving forward, sooner or later we can get a glimpse of the highway, can work our way towards it, and can find the onramp.

Time to start hacking. Move energy to create success.

On occasion, it is necessary to step back from our work (hacking), so that we can look to see our direction, to see if we have caught sight of the highway yet. If we don't see it yet, we get back into the thick of it and keep moving forward. When we do step back and see the highway, we make minor course corrections and get back to work.

Once we have made it to the onramp and have gotten onto the highway, our direction becomes clearer. Road signs allow us to change highways to get moving toward our desired destination. In other words, getting to the highway is the first step. We must then get our bearings and find the best highway to take us to our destination.

It is a matter of choice. The easiest choice is to do nothing. If we choose to do nothing, then there is no one to blame when we don't get anywhere. Desire without work grants us nothing. Work is required. Get to work.

The reward for work well done is the opportunity to do more.
— Jonas Salk

We either do or we don't get to work. Choice. Once we do get to work and find our way to the highway, that doesn't mean that it will all be smooth driving. We may come to a roadblock, or an accident that stops us. It is at that point that we must find a way to keep moving.

The critical thing is to keep going.

Create solutions. Think. Now that we have worked this hard to find the highway, we are practiced at finding solutions, and they are beginning to come to us in abundance.

We will fall into darkness upon occasion. We will go back to our old ways. Words like can't, try and want will invade when we have fallen back into our shadow.

We are now recognizing it for what it is and find our way back into the light. Follow the Invisible Truth and we WILL keep ourselves on the right path.

During the discussion of the nine laws and principles, Invisible Truth Alliance had meetings on a weekly basis amongst the leaders of the group to discuss where we were and how the company was developing. During discussions we talked about where we were with "working through our stuff."

I found this interesting. One of the team members had missed a few meetings in a row. We called her to find out what was going on. She stated that an event had happened in her life that had drawn negative energy to her and she had found herself dwelling on the negative. She "did not want to be a burden" in the meeting because she had realized that she was confronting her former shadow and had fallen into old patterns.

First, that she recognized that this is happening is a very positive thing. Second, this is the time when we most require ourselves to reach out to the helping hand that is always offered to the person who has a clear vision.

Keep moving forward. Understand that recognizing where we are at is being aware. Being aware is the first step of the entire process.

This reminds me of a story. There was a man stuck on his roof during the New Orleans flooding. One of his neighbors comes by in a rowboat and tells the guy to jump in so they can all get to safety. "Oh, no. God will save me. I am fine." A day later, the Coast Guard comes by in a ship because the waters were getting even higher and attempts to rescue the man from his rooftop. "No, I am fine…I have faith that God will save me." The next day, as the water is working its way up the roof, an Army helicopter comes by and tells the man to grab the ladder and climb to safety. He refuses the offer of help and sends the helicopter on its way.

The man drowns.

When he gets to heaven, he asks God…"Why did you forsake me? I had faith that you would save me and you let me perish!"…and God answered…"I did not forsake you. I sent a rowboat, a ship and a helicopter…."

Faith without work is dead. Saving ourselves requires work, and requires recognizing help.

My definition of success: to just keep moving in the right direction.

What is your definition of success?

Proverbs 12:14 From the fruit of his lips a man is filled with good things as surely as the work of his hands rewards him. (NIV)

Taking Responsibility

We must take personal responsibility for the excuses we choose. Once we take personal responsibility for these excuses, they lessen because we realize that they are nothing more than that…excuses. It is our choice; we can choose to beg during the harvest, or we can choose to be abundant. It is up to each one of us, individually.

Taking personal responsibility for our excuses is the first step in becoming aware.

Figuring out my priorities is the second step in becoming aware.

How does one eat an elephant? One bite at a time.

Consider this responsibility here. We are on the highway. Our presence at the destination is essential. We will not accept the potential consideration of a "slow down" becoming a "stop." Not even for a single moment. Our destination is the absolute manifestation of our ultimate joy; not for a moment do we accept the "slow down" and waver in the vision of us arriving to partake in the celebration. Success is the only option. This is the way to approach every day of our life. Every day.

Proverbs 13:4 The sluggard craves and gets nothing, but the desires of the diligent are fully satisfied. (NIV)

Desires do not gain abundance. Directed actions do. Directed action is energy in motion toward our desires.

Discipline. Diligence. Work.

When we choose to be diligent in work, directed energy flows. When directed energy flows, visions are manifested at an expedited rate. Remember, energy attracts like kind energy. As we move toward our goal, outside energy is added to the actions we are already taking, increasing the velocity and rate with which we are traveling toward our desired result.

Let's say I see a better way to accomplish a task at work that has been done the same way for years. I outline my thoughts and bring them to the bosses. They see the logic of my plan. The next thing I know, there are three departments working on my idea to set it in place. I carry the reward of recognition, and possibly of promotion.

A guy I know who works in the telecommunications business as a technician noticed an inefficiency in the way the company processed a certain action. This function, whatever it was, had been done the same way for years ("This is just the way we do it.") He brought it to the attention of the boss, in writing. Not only did he bring to the boss the inefficiency (problem), he brought to the boss a solution. The boss ran the idea "up the flagpole." My friend ended up saving this national company millions of dollars a year.

He was recognized at the company's national meeting and given a 50,000 dollar bonus and he was promoted.

This energy started with awareness (living in the now). The awareness created a thought. The thought led to talking with co-workers about the situation (words). The energy created by the group of coworkers created a positive reinforcement of the idea. He avoided the "nay-sayers" and focused his energy on the positive. The belief that there was a better way to do this function created a solution. The energy of the solution was brought to those who could create change in this function (work). The end result was my friend being in the position to purchase the home he had envisioned well ahead of his schedule.

Like kind energy attracts. This isn't just a philosophy. This is science in action.

The meaning of diligence is the constant, persistent and earnest effort to accomplish what is undertaken.

When we are diligent on a specific matter, we are focused. When we are focused on something, it becomes clear. When it is clear, we attract it.

By living in the now and being conscious of our actions at any given moment, we are creating positive energy in the universe…and doing God's work.

We are attracting it.

When we are persistent, specific and focused, with patience and time, we achieve our desired results in great abundance in our lives.

We are achieving our desired results today.

Proverbs 6:6-8 Go to the ant, you sluggard; consider its ways and be wise! It has no commander, no overseer or ruler, yet it

stores its provisions in summer and gathers its food at harvest. (NIV)

This is clear. We know what is required to bring us our desired result. We do it. We are our own guide, overseer and ruler.

Don't waste life in doubts and fears; spend yourself on the work before you, well assured that the right performance of this hour's duties will be the best preparation for the hours and ages that will follow it. — Ralph Waldo Emerson

Along the way, we will seek help, guidance and education, however that looks. What it does mean is that we control our own destinies by finding the help, education or leadership we require in order to continue on our path. When we take action, take responsibility and take control of our lives, we find those who will best help us to get to where we are going. Whether it is a school, a boss, a counseling session, a seminar, a friend…we find what it is that assists us, given the circumstance, and work toward manifesting the chosen result.

Proverbs 15:22 Plans fail for lack of counsel, but with many advisers they succeed. (NIV)

My Life's Work, My Job, Knowing the Difference

We all work for someone else. If we work for an employer, then we must work for them. We must show up on time, be where we are supposed to be when we are supposed to be there, and work with purpose. We do the very best job we can. When we own our own business, we work for the customer or the client…same rules apply.

We do our very best. We continue to strive towards being even better.

When we do work for others, it is essential that we realize that the work we are doing for others is a method through which we are creating our own destinies. When we have set our goals and have consciously decided that the work we do for others is a way in which we will realize our own vision, the work we do becomes a pleasure, not a burden.

I will repeat this. When I realize that the work I do for others is the work I do to realize my own vision...then work is no longer a burden, it is a means to an end. I am working to create my own vision.

The next thing that is essential to understand is that there is a difference between our life's work and a job. A job is, usually, a means to an end. For a few, their job is the vision that they have worked for and have manifested. At that point their job is no longer a job; it is their life's work. They are complete in that job and it is the fulfillment of their work.

To most of us a job is nothing more than just that. Some of us are satisfied with our job and are happy to be doing the tasks required to perform that job. These are the people prepared for the opportunity when it presents itself. They are qualified to take on the role that is offered them at the right time. If their vision goes no further than having this job, then they are fulfilled. There are not many who see their job as their life's vision.

Are we prepared to take on our desired role if it is presented to us today? Do we know the difference between our life's work and our job?

The next thing to be clear on is our vision. How can we get there if we do not know where we desire to be in the first place? Manifestation starts with the energy of creating a vision. It then works through the thoughts I have regarding that vision, which in turn is reflected in the words I use about that vision. I then move through the work required to bring my belief in line with that vision. Once I am clear, and once I believe in my vision, the work becomes almost effortless.

First, clarify our vision.

My work requires that I review that which has held me back in the past. As I am working my way though changing the thought patterns I have had around the issues in my life that have stopped me, new, precise, positive images will spur me to a better comprehension of where I desire to be.

This does not require psychoanalysis or counseling. However, in some cases, seeking counseling is a good idea, depending on how extreme the block is that is keeping me from doing the work toward my vision.

If I am an alcoholic, the first step in realizing my vision is to break my addiction. This could require help. If I were sadistically beaten as a child by an adult "close" to me, then I could require help. These may require outside help. Most of us do not carry the baggage of these extremes.

Be logical in our assessment of our "reasons" for our blockages.

In many cases, it is nothing more than changing the way we see things, changing our old neural pathways on how we react to external stimuli in our lives. Change comes to those who are aware of their circumstance and their standing within that circumstance. To objectively see what our circumstance is at any given moment is to be aware.

There are many heavily trodden paths in the way we see things, in our neural pathways. Forging a new path is nothing more than deciding to do so. Once we have chosen a new path, it is critical that we continue using the new path. Falling back into old patterns at the first sign of trouble on our new pathway is very easy.

This is a very important point. I will say it again. The reason most self-help teachings fail is because those being taught fall right back into old patterns at the first sign of trouble on their new pathway. Instead of finding a solution within the context of the new way they do things, they find it easier to fall back into old patterns.

Stay the course.

Success requires discipline. Discipline requires work. Work requires discipline.

Most courses focus on a few of the laws or principles and leave the rest out. With the laws and principles they did go over, the concepts were there but the details on how to make it work for us were not. By combining and practicing all nine of the laws and principles of Invisible Truth, we are able to...finally...combine all of the necessary teachings with our practical application.

Think of a way that YOU choose a new neural pathway today.

Let's continue with choosing the smooth highway over the road of thorns. When we come up on an accident on our new highway, instead of taking the first exit and getting lost behind the thorns again, think of another way to move forward. Maybe the thing to do is to help at the accident scene, whether that means helping those involved in the accident or pushing cars out of the way. Patience is the key here. We have hit a delay on our journey to where we are going, but we are not lost on the side streets, unable to see the highway.

There is no necessity to instinctively, reactively, abandon our pathway to our goal just because we're in that habit, on autopilot, and "we've always done it that way." Keep our vision in view. See the "flee" thoughts as they arise. Stay the course.

Seek a new solution in front of us.

The miraculous factor is the sudden emergence of a new plan, one which has never before occurred to us, such as taking the initiative and suggesting that we help push the cars out of the way. New, never before contemplated thoughts will appear from the brain we thought we were quite familiar with.

My Vision

My vision will become very clear. I will feel it, smell it, taste it. I will know how it makes me feel...how I choose for it to make me feel. A vision is not a thought. It is a solid picture of where I am headed and how it makes me feel when I am there. Once I have cleared my blocks from making that vision a reality, I will work towards doing what's necessary in order to realize that vision.

It is my solid picture. Mine.

It is not enough to think that we would like to have something in our life.

Work is a law and principle we will not ignore. Many avoid work because the word itself is associated with effort. Well, what else do we have to do that is so important? How are we going to set out and accomplish our goals without effort?

We are going to work, one way or the other. Either we work to maintain our "want," or we work toward our desired vision. The choice is ours.

When we have a clearly stated vision, work becomes effortless. We know where we are going and delight in the journey to get there.

How many times have we heard "it's not the destination, it's the journey"...or a version of that statement?

Again, it all comes back to choice. I could choose not to learn this principle about work. However, it is essential that I understand that directed action is a key component to receiving abundance in my life, regardless of the type of abundance I am striving for.

I can sit on the couch and think and speak about being rich. If I do nothing about it, then, chances are riches will elude me. If I do get rich by, say, hitting the lotto, then chances are even greater that those riches will escape me because I have done no work to earn them, learn about them, or find out how to handle them.

Work is directed, focused energy which distinctly follows our thoughts, words and beliefs...towards our vision.

At this point we may still be dismissing this principle...the principle of work. We may be saying to ourselves, "I have worked hard my entire life and I can't seem to get ahead." I suggest that we keep studying...as one or more of the laws and principles have been left out of our strategy.

The other thing to look at is this: what have we worked hard at? A job or our vision?

We feel we have worked hard all our life, but never believed that we would get ahead. Well, we have received exactly what we thought we would. Our vision was fulfilled.

Congratulations on our ability to manifest. Would we like to rephrase our thoughts now? Go ahead...the world is waiting.

I would not live in a house where the builder skipped two of the nine steps in the building of that house. If I designed a house with two bathrooms and got an outhouse instead, I would not be happy. However, if I did not work hard and pay for those two bathrooms, then I have no right to them, and I will have to live with the outhouse. If I work hard enough to get those bathrooms, but the house didn't have a roof, what good is that going to do me?

To continue on with the construction analogy, we all know that the key to a successful building or home is a good foundation. The laws and principles of Invisible Truth set out to help give us the building blocks of that solid foundation. From there, the thoughts, words, work and belief in our vision will finish the construction we desire.

Our vision is realized as we become aware of the work necessary to attain that vision. As we work towards that vision, the energy of the universe leads us to increased energy toward our goal through the laws of attraction.

Become aware. Create a vision. Think in positive terms about that vision. Speak of how we are working toward that vision. Believe in the vision, work toward it, and that vision unburdens itself. Yes, there is effort, but the effort becomes joyful. Work then becomes play.

The point is this. All nine laws and principles are required in our strategy in order to get to where we are going.

What work I have done I have done because it has been play. If it had been work I shouldn't have done it. Who was it who said, "Blessed is the man who has found his work?" Whoever it was he has the right idea in his mind. Mind you, he says his work--not somebody else's work. The work that is really a man's own work is play and not work at all. Cursed is the man who has found some other man's work and cannot lose it. When we talk about great workers of the world we really mean the great players of the world. The fellows who groan and sweat under the weary load of toil that they bear never can hope to do anything great. How can they when their souls are in a ferment of revolt against the employment of their hands and brains? The product of slavery, intellectual or physical, can never be great. — Mark Twain

This is good news. When all nine laws and principles are used in conjunction with each other, work becomes a relaxed action. The stress of work dissipates. One of life's worries becomes nullified. When we have a clear vision of what we are working towards, the effort of the work unburdens itself.

I will say this again. In order for work to unburden itself, we must create a vision of that towards which we are working. The vision we have must be clear. We must see it, feel it, smell it, and in our minds, be able to touch it. With clear strong visions, comes belief. With belief, comes work. I no longer have a job; I have my work...a means to an end. Work becomes play.

A visionary is someone who knows where they are going, no matter what. Are we visionaries?

Work becomes a relaxed action because the confidence, belief and faith we have in the manifestation we are creating fill our bucket to overflowing with pristine water and with overflowing goodness. We see our lives as fulfilled, abundant and with purpose. We have a vision we are working towards and our work toward that vision is with purpose. We are living within the divine powers of God, the laws of nature, and the universe. This is taking the highway, the easy route.

When we find the highway, we find the inner stillness and complete peace of our connection with the universe, with God.

Galatians 6:7-10 Do not be deceived: God cannot be mocked. A man reaps what he sows. The one who sows to please his sinful nature, from that nature will reap destruction; the one who sows to please the Spirit, from the Spirit will reap eternal life. Let us not become weary in doing good, for at the proper time we will reap a harvest if we do not give up. Therefore, as we have opportunity, let us do good to all people, especially to those who belong to the family of believers. (NIV)

Action Steps for the Week

- I work toward creating my vision every day, in order to unburden myself from work being a chore. My vision is flexible, but the context within which it is set is not.

- I find what information I must have to do the work I wish to do, in order to move towards my vision. (I live in the now. I learn new information with a positive attitude, with the certainty that I *can* learn it, that I *can easily* learn it.)

- I work at learning the tools that are necessary to perform the task I must accomplish next. (I choose to see my vision foremost in my mind. When murky water drifts in front of it, I'll calmly replace that hose with the pristine one.)

- I set my vision quite high and recognize that the steps I accomplish along my way are just steps, not the vision itself.

- I share my vision with others in order to receive help in achieving my vision, as well as to reinforce my vision within myself. (I feel gratitude for that help; I am always thankful.)

- I work diligently to accomplish the things I have set for myself.

- I work to find the blocks in my path. I will then choose to find a new way to think and speak about what it is that I choose to manifest. With my change in speech and thought comes a new belief.

- I remain aware of the discipline necessary to manifest my desired results.

- I remain disciplined in my work toward my vision.

- I grasp my vision clearly, feeling all there is to feel in that vision. Work becomes effortless as I work toward that vision.

Law and Principle # 6

Being Thankful

Life isn't a dress rehearsal...this is it. — Unknown

In all ways, we are thankful. Even when my bucket overflows with negative stuff, I will be thankful. I am alive. For that, I am thankful. When the end comes and I am facing "the discovery of the real secret," I will be thankful. Until that time comes, I am thankful for all that I have, all that I have had the opportunity to give to this life, and all that it has taught me.

Let us rise up and be thankful, for if we didn't learn a lot today, at least we learned a little, and if we didn't learn a little, at least we didn't get sick, and if we did get sick, at least we didn't die; so, let us all be thankful. — Buddha

To the best of my knowledge, I have got one shot at this life as I know it. I am giving this one life all I have. That means doing and saying the right thing, and being grateful for what I have. I am not getting out of this deal alive, and I know it. The best I can do is always better than I am doing right now. I strive to better my best at all times. What else do I have to do that is so important, that will allow me to live one minute longer anyway?

When I get to the end of this journey, and I come face to face with myself, what is it that I wish to see? I am grateful for the opportunity to do the right thing and be the best me I can be. I am not going to *try* to be the best I can be. I am being the best I can be.

Sometimes the lessons have been tough. As the old saying goes, "Nothing is sure in life but death and taxes." The difference is that we know what taxes are all about and how much the government says I owe. No one knows what death brings. Those who claim they know what happens after we die are stating their own conclusion. I am thankful for my life. The end of life as I know it is coming soon enough. For those of us with enough years behind us, it is pretty amazing how fast the time has gone.

Being thankful is a positive energy. Being thankful brings on positive words. Being thankful brings on positive emotion. The positive energy that is brought out with being thankful draws to us that energy that vibrates at the same positive levels.

A lack of gratitude manifests want. When we are not thankful, we focus on things that we don't have. When we focus on not having, then we attract not having into our life.

Sometimes being thankful is a bit of a stretch. When there are things going on in my life that hurt me and those around me, it is tough to be thankful. That is the test. I have seen those who have wallowed in self-pity, a negative energy. At times in my life I have been one of those people. Self-pity is a negative emotion which in turn brings a vibration that is very similar. That does not mean that sorrow isn't real. That does not mean that anguish isn't real. They are. I can tell you this: "I have had the hardest life of anyone I know...except for everyone else." It is important when we are at the very depths of our sorrow or anguish or dilemma (or an albatross composed of all three), that we find a thing to be thankful for.

I remember being in the depths of sorrow for the death of a loved one when, for a moment, I wasn't sure I wished to go on. It was then that I raised my eyes to the sky and thanked the Lord for the ability to feel such powerful emotions. That was the best I could do at the time.

As time passed, the world began to fall more into focus. I began to move again. Life kept going. Eventually, I found a reason to smile again. Laughter came. I again was able to give thanks for the love that I had felt, and still did feel, for the departed loved one. What a treasure they had been in my life. I was thankful for the joy they had brought me. That, in turn, made me realize my responsibility to bring joy to others.

Everybody's lives are different. Some people have grown up in good homes with good parents and some people have grown up in a much tougher situation.

Regardless of where we came from, what is happening to us right now is a direct result of what materials we put into our bucket. My bucket is nothing more than what I have created in my past and it overflows with all that I have put into it. If I continue to put mud into my bucket, then that is what is coming out...mud.

Remember, how we react to the world is largely molded by the time we are around six years old. The emotions of the pain inflicted upon us, by others, was more powerful than the joy and pain we felt as children ourselves. Our patterns became set. Our subconscious mind became a reactionary unit.

The point of this is that we can retrain our minds to think and to react in a different way than our childhood experiences have taught us. First, we must become aware of the thought processes we go through. Much of the time we have no real idea why we react the way we do to a specific stimulus. Much of it comes from our childhood. If we look at why we react the way we do, then we can change it.

Look at our most basic reactions. Take a really hard look.

My mother had a deathly fear of snakes. She would go into an uncontrollable panic at the sight, or even hint, of a snake anywhere near her or in the same county or same state as her. I mean, it was bad. I once asked her what this fear was all about, after she tried to rip my hair out getting past me at the sight of a six inch garter snake. She didn't know.

Gramps was still alive so I asked him. He chuckled and told me that Mom's sisters were upset with her for telling on them, so they put a few garter snakes in her bed, under the covers. Mom was about five. When she got into bed it scared her very badly and her sisters laughed at her.

Well, there it was, a lifetime set up for a deathly fear of snakes. Once I brought this information back to Mom, she began to remember. She decided right there that she would react differently when she saw a snake again. There was still some fear, but it was no longer irrational. Her reaction was no longer hysterical. She didn't fall in love with snakes, but her reaction was not nearly as extreme.

"It was no longer irrational...."

Look at the way we react to the world. Is there a reason that we react in a certain way to certain things that isn't really rational? Find out what it is. When the reason why is discovered, be grateful for the discovery. That, by itself, begins the process of change. Stop and take a look at this now. What is the most irrational thing that we do that *seems* to be out of our control?

For all things, be grateful.

It is vitally important, especially when I am going through hard times, that I be thankful. That is when I am most vulnerable to the negative vibration tendencies that could, if I allow it, bring additional negative into my life. Remember the old saying "when it rains, it pours?" Why do you think that is? The patterns of our lives have been set. If we give in to the negative patterns we have learned, then it is going to attract more negative.

It's the old "snowball" effect.

The other lesson to be learned here is this: when things are not going very well, I have the potential to fall into the trap of the "victim" mentality. If we become ungrateful, there is a tendency to blame others. As soon as I begin blaming others, I begin to wallow in the "victim" mentality, which starts a muddy evolution toward circling the drain.

Some of us just like to wallow in the mire of the mess we have made of our lives, hoping that, consciously or subconsciously, someone will feel sorry for us. At least in that way we will be getting attention. If this sounds like it is hitting just a little too close to home, then it is time to change it to a positive. Time to turn it around. Start with implementing the lessons taught in this book.

This "victim" pattern is often very hard to detect. When bad things would happen to me, I would often get compliments about how well I managed in crisis. Subconsciously, I was getting the attention that I "wanted." It wasn't until I stood back and asked myself why I attracted these negative things into my life that I began to break the pattern.

Mom used to call those actions "attention getting devices."

For years it seemed my motto was "Can't you see how hard I try?" This is a statement of very low vibration. Change it…now. No one cares about what we "tried" to do. What people care about is what we did, or for that matter, didn't do.

When it is time…cry. Cry hard. Feel all the emotions that come from the bad thing that has happened in our lives. When it is time to stop…STOP. Raise up and move on. As we move on, be especially grateful for that which we mourn. It was a good thing in our life, realize it…and keep moving. If that thing that we mourn was not a good thing in our life, we would not be mourning it. (Either the arrival, the having or the departure was a good thing, a powerful thing. Mourning does not occur lightly.) When it is time, be grateful for that thing, or that person, that has been in our life, then get up and keep moving.

Get up.

I remember, during one of the seminars I attended, the facilitator gave his definition of success: to just keep going. Somehow this resonated with me. Intellectually I made every effort to break down this statement. After a number of years I came to my own definition of success: to just keep going in the right direction. "To just keep going" had the potential to allow me to fall into the victim mentality again. (Can't you see how hard I try?) I have decided that I choose to be seen by how well I do, not how hard I "try."

Just keep going in the right direction.

Work toward good things. When we do the "now" correctly, the future takes care of itself in a positive way. What we do right now is what our bucket overflows with later. Allow the negative to flow out. The more positive that we put into the bucket, the sooner the negative is washed out. The positive starts with our thoughts. It is backed by the words we speak, which in turn reinforce what we believe. Then, work towards the vision we have created, while being grateful for all that we have.

These things we keep in mind while handling the thing that is before us, right now…this moment. Put into place that which we believe, and work on it right this moment to bring to us the result we desire. Deal with the now…now. These concepts appear to be very simple. Do not be fooled. This is a conscious, lifelong process. Breaking the negative patterns of our lives requires ongoing, never ending vigilance, diligence and discipline.

Just keeping going in the right direction.

When I push against something, it pushes back. When I continue to fight something, it fights back. I now choose to go with the flow, to not fight it. I change the direction of the flow of energy.

One of my favorite examples of this principle of energy came from my children's dojo where they were learning Aikido at the ripe old age of six. The art of Aikido uses the flow of the body (energy) coming at us, to change the direction of our attacker's flow of energy to our advantage. It is hard to describe other than that.

When done properly, it almost looks like a dance. Watching the senseis performing during their demonstrations was really something special. The point of the discipline is not to hurt, but to control and defuse a situation, and to change it to our advantage. It is mesmerizing. I choose to be thankful for the lessons I have learned by studying my children's lessons in Aikido. I have learned an invaluable lesson for life.

Redirect the flow of the energy.

Here is a side note to this story. Though the kids were very young when they studied Aikido (for about four years), and both claim they don't really remember any of their training, it made a large difference in one of my children's lives. While attending college in San Francisco, my daughter was standing inside a very crowded train (Bay Area Rapid Transit) on the way to her job. She was standing right next to one of the doors.

When the door opened, a man exited the train at a somewhat deserted platform. As the man exited, he turned and grabbed my daughter by the arm, attempting to drag her out of the train. Her instinct allowed her to take the man's motion and turn it against him in a way that when the automatic doors shut, they shut on his head and he reacted by jerking his hand and head free as the train began to move. When asked about it, she will say that she was lucky.

Luck: when preparation meets opportunity. How have we prepared ourselves?

Look past the challenge to the positive end result. Given certain circumstances, at times this appears impossible. Nothing is impossible. Sometimes the best we can do is "make the best of a bad situation." When dealing with the challenge of our life, the sooner it gets behind us, the better.

If I am sick and I think, focus and speak of the illness, if I concentrate on fighting it and I consume my whole life with the sickness and the stress that it brings on, I create more of that sickness.

Look past the sickness, and think, focus and speak of being well. Work toward being well by eating properly and working the regimen provided by our healthcare practitioners with wellness in mind.

Our action is a relaxed action because of the calm confidence and belief, or faith, in the manifestation of wellness. This is achieved through the utilization of the Invisible Truth.

I am thankful and grateful that it is my choice to be able to change my direction. No matter how bad it seems right now, I can choose to change the direction I am heading.

Psalms 118:1 Give thanks to the Lord, for he is good; his love endures forever. (NIV)

Psalms 118:5 In my anguish I cried to the Lord, and he answered me by setting me free. (NIV)

Give thanks for the mercy of the universe. Especially when the weight of our decisions have fallen upon us and the pressure seems unbearable.

We can live in the now and be fully aware and fully conscious. Do the now correctly. Tap into that divine power of God; we will be answered, and set in a better place.

Unlimited abundance awaits us. Be thankful.

1 Thessalonians 5:16-18 Be joyful always; pray continually; give thanks in all circumstances, for this is God's will for you in Christ Jesus. (NIV)

Prayer comes in many forms. It starts with thought. In our thoughts, we are grateful. We give thanks for all we have. I choose not to focus on what I don't have. I have written this book with the emphasis on Christian values, the things I have studied through my faith. We can each find the words of our own religion, our own belief. They are there.

I had the opportunity to meet a very inspirational woman named Helen Thayer. She is an adventurer. Among the many adventures she has had was being the first woman to walk to the North Pole. She did this without the benefit of a dogsled or snowmobile. When prompted, she told of some of the harrowing situations she found herself in during some of her adventures. With these stories she would always include her version of her "emergency prayer." Her prayer, whenever she found herself in a perilous situation, was "I need you now, God." She had said it so many times that it was abbreviated to "Now, God." Prayer comes in all forms.

Regardless of the circumstance, regardless of the outcome, whatever happened, she was grateful.

The energy of the universe is mysterious; unlock the mysteries with the Invisible Truth. The energy that flows through it has common threads with the principles of most all of the faiths of the world. Energy has direction. The redirection of that energy is controlled by us. This is a common thread in the various philosophies, faiths and laws of the universe.

When I realized this, it was empowering.

In everything, give thanks. I give thanks in everything, because as I focus on things that I choose to have in my life, I follow the laws and principles taught here. When I choose to follow the Invisible Truth, the Universe and my God begin to open the doors of manifestation.

If I lose something in my life, I am making room for something else, and I am grateful. When something comes into my life, even if it is not what I desired, I am grateful. I will look at what has

come into my life and understand that it is something that the
energy of the universe has brought to me so that I can learn from it.
I find the result I desire, given the circumstance, focus on it and
begin to create it through my action of the moment.

There is a reason for everything. This is where the laws of the
universe tie to the principles of faith. Cause and effect. They go
hand in hand.

Being thankful allows us to see the opportunities in our failures or
in our mistakes that we would not otherwise see. It opens our eyes
to the possibilities inherent in any situation.

*Gratitude unlocks the fullness of life. It turns what we have into
enough, and more. It turns denial into acceptance, chaos into
order, confusion into clarity...It turns problems into gifts, failures
into success, the unexpected into perfect timing, and mistakes into
important events. Gratitude makes sense of our past, brings peace
for today and creates a vision for tomorrow.*
— Melody Beattie

*There are two ways to live your life. One is as though nothing is a
miracle. The other is as though everything is a miracle.*
— Albert Einstein

When I was younger, I was taught that it is all in the hands of God.
I interpreted that to mean that whatever happened to me was God's
will. That just didn't resonate with me. It just didn't. To me that
meant that I was a permanent victim. Whatever God willed for me,
so be it. I fought this until I discovered a teacher who helped me
realize that it **was** God's will. God's will was right there in the
Bible. His will was that I be grateful that I had control over the
direction of my life. God gave us freewill.

God gave us freewill. There is no single, more essential concept in
all of religion, except to love our neighbor.

God gave us freewill. This has been interpreted as meaning we can
do it His way or our way...and our ways are wrong. Let's look at

this differently. We were made in His likeness. We choose to perform the work ourselves, following His teachings. That is freewill. It is my choice to do things the right way. God is within me. Doing things the right way is doing things God's way.

God is within me. I might as well let Him out.

Write a list of all of the things that we are thankful for. When a negative thought or moment arises, say thank you for the present moment and for all of the things on our lists. Be thankful for the negative moment, because it gave us the opportunity to look at that negative moment and correct it.

The list can be anything. Thank you for the clothes that I wear. Thank you for the food to eat. Thank you for the people in my life. Thank you for my health. Thank you for all that I have. Thank you for self-awareness and positive energy…for the desire to be positive and to have a healthy influence on those around me…for the power to exact change upon my world and our world…for the burning desire to conceive of a community of emotionally strong and mentally healthy people, and for the tenacity to initiate this.

Our vision allows us to be clear on what we are thankful for.

In all things be thankful.

Gratitude is the memory of the heart. — French Proverb

Action Steps for the Week

- Be aware of our work habits and change them if necessary. Work is energy in motion and energy is potential force, inherent power, capacity for doing work and the ability to cause change. Work is the foundation to abundance. Be thankful for our work.

- Make a list of 25 things that we are thankful about. No matter how small, write it down.

- Become conscious of negative thoughts and moments, and immediately give thanks for the things on our list. Redirect negative to positive energy.

- Read our lists periodically. Add to it. Give thanks in everything, and we begin to replace the ungratefulness and lack with thankfulness and abundance.

Gratitude is the sign of noble souls. — Aesop

Law and Principle # 7

Forgiveness

The weak can never forgive. Forgiveness is an attribute of the strong. — Mahatma Gandhi

Forgiveness is a necessity. Without it we will never find peace, nor will we ever be able to manifest the positive into our lives. Striving to forgive all in our lives for every wrong or slight, whether perceived or actual, is something that we will do every day. We clear the path through our forgiveness of ourselves and of others.

Forgiveness means giving up all hope for a better past.
— Lily Tomlin

Though spoken by a comedian, this point is one that we must understand. Resentment of our past is holding us back from the treasures of the future. Acceptance of our sins and forgiveness of our past is critical to creating the positive lives we are making for ourselves.

A sin is defined as a transgression of divine law, or any act that is considered a willful or deliberate violation of a religious or moral principle. It is also any reprehensible and deliberate action or behavior which causes fault or offense. A sin is the action we took that we had to think about. We failed to do the right thing. Remember, the wrong thing is the one we had to think about. We all know, instinctively, what the right thing to do is.

Forgiving Ourselves

Forgiveness of ourselves is critical to moving forward. That does not give us an avenue on which we can keep sinning. Just because we forgive ourselves does not mean that society must forgive us. Evil is evil...period.

We know the difference between right and wrong. As long as we consciously continue to strive to do the right thing, our occasional blunder will be forgiven. We correct that which we have done, seek the forgiveness of those we have wronged, and move forward with our lives in a positive way.

When we tap into our God, universal or logical consciousness, instinct takes over.

Forgiving Others

When we don't forgive others, we harbor the experience of what someone did to us. We live in the past, and live the experience over and over in our minds. This creates a block to our moving forward in bringing to ourselves all that we are capable of manifesting. It blocks our karma, as it were, by not allowing anything past the stop we have put in front of us. It creates darkness in our souls that will not come to the light until we become determined to drag it out, kicking and screaming, exposing it for the poison that it is.

Confront the dark parts of yourself, and work to banish them with illumination and forgiveness. Your willingness to wrestle with your demons will cause your angels to sing. Use the pain as fuel, as a reminder of your strength. — August Wilson

I find myself thinking about the slights, or wrongs, I feel I have had perpetrated against me, by family, by friends, by business associates, by companies. I used to think about them before I went to sleep. Sometimes I was thinking about them when I woke up. I spent my time thinking about how "I would get them back," or what I would say to them, etc. We have all done it. Admitting to myself that I held a grudge, that I was resentful of things or people in my life, was the first step in allowing me to be free of that negative feeling.

When we hold a grudge, the only one who we are hurting is ourselves. The negative energy we use in the poisonous thoughts we have regarding the wrong done to us, in turn, brings to us the negative vibration that we are emanating to the world. The vibration of the energy that we are moving in attracts like vibration. Remember, thought is energy. Thought is very powerful. We are becoming aware of not only what we think about, but how we think about it.

Before you embark on a journey of revenge, dig two graves.
— Confucius

Hatred is the coward's revenge for being intimidated.
— George Bernard Shaw

Again, whether I am obsessing on the past or plotting the future around the wrong, perceived or actual, I have created a block that stops the power of creation that I am striving to achieve. Forgiveness allows the block to melt, moving us forward to achieve our goals in this life.

Without forgiveness, there is no future.
— Desmond Tutu

When we think, focus and meditate on things in our past or our future, our brain sends signals throughout our body as if it is happening right now. The emotions and the energy of those emotions run through us. We can take it into our subconscious state as is evident in dreaming. Our buckets become muddy again.

When we do this, we find ourselves in a place of worry, fear and anger which can cause panic attacks, high blood pressure and numerous mental and physical health problems over something that is not there. It is not happening right now. It is not happening in the moment I am living right now. Yet, our random, compulsive thoughts are unnecessarily creating self-infliction, self-fear and self-suffering which develop undesired realities in our lives.

To forgive is to set a prisoner free and discover that the prisoner is you. — Lewis B. Smedes

Forgive, and live in the now. When someone does something wrong to me, instead of seeking revenge, I shall focus on moving forward. Concentrate on the positive. Let our bucket overflow with goodness.

That does not mean that the injustice is ignored. Sometimes the injustice is inconsequential, thereby easily dismissed. Sometimes the injustice is unconscious; the one doing me wrong has no idea that a wrong is being done, at which point it is usually just a matter of pointing it out. Sometimes the injustice is perceived, and with communication the value of the perceived injustice is detected after the fact; a simple apology should ensue.

Sometimes, but rarely, the injustice is real, purposeful and spiteful. These are the tricky ones. If the injustice has done us physical, emotional or monetary damage, getting over it can be a bit of a stretch. However, remember to consider the source. If someone has done us wrong, with intent, then they especially are the ones who require our forgiveness. They are the ones locked in their own stuff. Not only is forgiveness the right thing to do, it is the best revenge. They will not know how to react to forgiveness as they are gearing up for a fight and their minds are boiling over with their attack and defense plans...a very negative and dark place. However, forgiveness must be genuine, or it is not forgiveness at all.

Mathew 7:1-2 Do not judge, or you too will be judged. For in the same way you judge others, you will be judged, and with the measure you use, it will be measured to you. (NIV)

All major religious traditions carry basically the same message, that is love, compassion and forgiveness...the important thing is that they should be part of our daily lives. — Dalai Lama

To understand everything is to forgive everything. — Buddha

The people who touch our lives, at whatever level, no matter how significant, do the things they do for reasons that we may never clearly understand. As Buddha said, if we understood everything, we would forgive everything. The point is this, what is done is done. We may never understand, however, we can forgive. Many times those who wronged us feel regret and are truly seeking forgiveness. The power of forgiveness is huge. Do not underestimate it.

Understand the vibrational magnitude of that which we feel. It is powerful. It comes back to us.

Let our Supreme Being and the Universe do the judging. It is my belief that when it comes time to move to the other side, the first one I have to face is me. I know who else I will be answering to, but I am sure that I will answer to myself first. The divine power I answer to is the one I was born with, that God told me was within me. My sin against God is not performing His work that He had given me the power to do.

Indeed, after centuries of successful cleansings, even the Catholic Church itself has renamed the sacrament of confession (penance) the "Sacrament of Reconciliation" in order to re-emphasize the healing and the return of the repentant to a clear conscience and the graces of God.

I know the difference between right and wrong. Consciously performing the wrong act is a sin. I will have to answer for it...to me first. It could be that the anguish I would feel at the end of my life is the turmoil I have felt throughout my life multiplied into a single event...the end of life as I know it...knowing that I was consciously doing the wrong things my entire life. That, to me, sounds like Hell.

The converse is also true. Knowing the difference between right and wrong, and always striving to do the right thing, my conscience is clear. When it comes time for me to face myself and my God, I will be satisfied that I have done all in my power to make this a better world. The energy I take into the next realm is clean. Heaven?

Sometimes the one who has wronged us…is us. Recognizing that we have done wrong is a challenge to the ego, whether that wrong was done to others or to ourselves. When we recognize that we have done wrong, there are two individuals we should seek forgiveness from, the one who has been wronged and ourselves.

Make amends. Admit fault. Seek forgiveness. Forgiveness may not be granted. I forgive myself and move on.

Though it is right for me to seek redemption from the one who I have wronged, it is for them to grant it. If they choose not to, then I have done what is right and it is time to clear my path of this obstacle. Choose to stay focused on the positive.

On occasion, our error, as righteously intended as it is, is simply wrong because we did not have all the information necessary for the situation. We did not fully understand the circumstance, and we came to an erroneous conclusion. It happens. There are many examples I can think of in my life, and I am sure we all can. Understand the error, seek forgiveness from those we have wronged and forgive ourselves. Move on.

People find it far easier to forgive others for being wrong than being right. — JK Rowling

Remember the old adage "To err is human, to forgive, divine." Taking that one step further…

To forgive is human, to forget divine. — James Grand

Romans 12:21 Do not be overcome by evil, but overcome evil with good. (NIV)

The Universe and our Supreme Being will take care of it, so that we can continue to fill our bucket with good things to overflow into our lives. Let it be. Move on to good.

When evil enters our world, the first thing we will do is examine why this evil has entered our world. Take the appropriate actions in the situation without lowering ourselves to the level of the evil which has appeared. Correct the reason the evil entered our world in the first place. Forgive those who have sinned against us...and move on.

Psalms 54:5-7 Let evil recoil on those that slander me; in your faithfulness destroy them. I will sacrifice a freewill offering to you; I will praise your name, O Lord, for it is good. For he has delivered me from my troubles, and my eyes have looked in triumph on my foes. (NIV)

There is a reason we have heard all the old sayings. They have a truth in them that is both universal law and scriptural law. "What goes around comes around." Remember that one? We put into the world positive energy, we get positive energy, and vice versa. This biblical verse from Psalms confirms, scripturally, what science has already shown us. To me, this verse is telling me to leave the judgment to God, to the universe, to whatever our faith declares.

Our enemy (those who sinned against us) will get what is coming to them, through the negative energy they put out. I have let the judgment go (positive energy), forgiven my enemies (positive energy), and looked at the situation with favor as I have acted above those who have wronged me (positive energy). Forgiveness allows the positive energy to attract more positive energy.

Most have heard the phrase "Vengeance is mine, saith the Lord." That comes out of Romans 12:19. It is a saying that we have heard whether we were raised in a Christian environment, or church experience, or not. It is another reminder for us to let it go. Let the world (the universe) take care of itself...just tend to our own stuff.

The universal laws of cause and effect are written, quite clearly, into biblical scripture. If we actually spend time listening to someone (open our ears and stop thinking about how we are going to respond), a person's reaction towards almost any stimulus becomes predictable, based on the laws of attraction. The tone that one emanates from their very being is reflected in the way they speak, which is a reflection of the way they think, what they believe and how they view the world.

Once we become adept at hearing not only the words spoken, but also how they are delivered, as well as the actions and the reactions to the daily stimuli of those who are speaking to us, we can decipher the message as being either negative or positive. We do this through their words, their presentation, and also of the background they came from. Most psychics are nothing more than people who are good at reading others, their tone, words and body language. Practice. Get a little psychic ourselves. It also allows us to determine the underlying state of energy of each person in our lives, be it positive or negative. Life becomes easier when I know with whom I wish to surround myself.

Forgiveness Is Unlimited

Matthew 18:21-22 Then Peter came to Jesus and asked, "Lord, how many times shall I forgive my brother when he sins against me? Up to seven times?"

Jesus answered, "I tell you, not seven times, but seventy-seven times." (NIV)

This is saying that we are to forgive over and over again. Forgiveness is unlimited.

Knowing that, we can still forgive someone and move out of a bad situation. Just because we forgave someone does not mean that we have to hang around for more punishment from them or anyone else. Remember, people become predictable. "Fool me once, shame on you. Fool me twice, shame on me." Or, as my son says, "Come on, dude, get a clue."

Be wise. It is okay to remove ourselves from a toxic atmosphere or from an individual who continually creates physical or mental problems for us.

The key is to love. Remember, in all things love is always appropriate. When I forgive and love, I attract more love and happiness into my own life.

When I forgive and live in the now, I let go of the negative and look to the positive. Abundance abounds. Now that I have forgiven others with love in my heart, there is one more individual to forgive.

That is me.

I have spoken with many, many people and have found that their biggest challenge was to forgive themselves. They have done something, and then they have held on to the guilt. Guilt has this nonstop ability to eat away at someone from the inside out. Guilt is one of, if not the strongest of, the emotions that can truly harm. Guilt creates an enemy from within. It has the ability to create illness, (dis-ease) both physically and emotionally. Carrying guilt fills our bucket.

I do not say that lightly. Some may feel "dis-ease," then psychosomatic pains (that which stems from the mind), and then more pain and agony (those actions that Mom called "attention getting devices"). Then, actual physical and mental illness may follow. It has been scientifically proven beyond a shadow of a doubt that "Stress kills."

The art of being yourself at your best is the art of unfolding your personality into the person you want to be...Be gentle with yourself, learn to love yourself, to forgive yourself, for only as we have the right attitude toward ourselves can we have the right attitude toward others. — Wilfred Peterson

In most cases the sincere, honest apology dissolves the anger I caused with my wrongdoing. There are times when it does not. This is when the apology includes a few more steps, after which each party can make a truthful evaluation of whether the apology worked or not. Then each person can choose whether or not to resume the relationship.

This extra step exists in many organized groups. Here are a few examples. In traditional churches like the Catholic Church, a parishioner confesses (lets go of) his sins. The priest listens, gives God's forgiveness and blessing and says, "Do your penance (usually saying a number of prayers), and go forth and sin no more."

In Alcoholics Anonymous, steps four through ten specifically spell out the making amends steps necessary to gain forgiveness from others as well as ourselves.

These same steps can be paraphrased from "new churches" like the Church of Scientology as "Make up the damage done...apply for re-entry to the group...."

Even our moms made us do these steps. "Tell your sister you're sorry. Now, help her pick those dolls up and put them all back the way they were." Of course, that was usually followed with something like "or you'll get no dessert." We are free to create the consequence of our actions. Freedom to, not freedom from.

Sounds straightforward to me. "...Confess your sins...Accept God's forgiveness...Make amends...Make up the damage done...And go forth and sin no more."

When the harmful action cannot be washed clean with a simple apology, add in these steps. Be sincere and complete in admitting the entire sin; holding onto any of it just causes it to remain with us forever. Ensure that we accept forgiveness from ourselves also; let it go. Make up for it.

Why should the person forgive us without us having to return the money we stole? Why should we be forced to forgive them without them returning our property to us? The laws of the universe, science and man stand behind this also. Karma defines it. The laws of man were strictly designed to balance the books to the best that man is able. Some books just cannot be balanced.

Enact a logical plan. Add in no revenge, vengeance nor hatred. Make amends, no more, no less; that is what we owe. Use our own judgment to define what we owe. We are neither a victim nor a martyr; we do not owe them forever, nor do they own us. Be honest and thorough in fulfilling our duty to them and to ourselves on this.

When "our job here is done," then we are done. Finished. "Go forth and sin no more." We are not branded as a horrible being unless we brand ourselves by not letting go. Go forward into the light. Learn from this. Be good. Attract goodness. And live in the now by letting this go.

...There must be something to this. If so many great and varied groups have perfected their own form of the same ideal, then it has merit. And it has withstood the test of time.

We have defined sin and apology. The natural thing to do is to now define repentance.

Repent: to feel sorry, self-reproachful or contrite for a past conduct; regret or be conscience-stricken about past action, attitude, etc. To feel such sorrow for sin or fault as to be disposed to change one's life for the better.

To repent: to take the dirty hose out of our bucket and put the clean hose in.

Forgive: to grant pardon and cease feeling resentment against.

To forgive: clean water. To ask forgiveness: more clean water.

Our bucket overflows with pristine water. The dirt has been purged away. Good is flowing in our life. We have been cleansed, pardoned or spared.

The concept is simple. Fill our bucket with dirty water and the bucket overflows dirt into our life.

Change the hose to pristine water and our bucket, once the dirt has flowed out, overflows into our life with pristine water.

Put the dirty hose back in, and the dirt overflows out. Put the pristine back in, and the pristine flows out. Put the dirty hose back in and the dirt flows out. Put the pristine back in and the cycle continues. Simple as that.

And that is why forgiveness is endless. I choose to follow the Invisible Truth and watch great things overflow in my life. If I mess up and put the dirty hose back in for a moment, it is okay; I will repent by asking forgiveness of others and myself, thereby putting the clean hose back in my bucket and letting the good water flow.

If I am not sincere in my repentance, then it is important to identify why. By blocking my repentance, I am blocking my positive energy and it might actually be time to seek counseling.

When I continue to focus on the negative that I may have created, and I let that negative harbor inside of me, I attract more of the very thing that I regret into my life.

Forgive others, forgive ourselves. Love ourselves. Do the right thing.

There is no love without forgiveness, and there is no forgiveness without love. — Bryant H. McGill

The past is the past. To dwell on the past creates what I dwell on, and it becomes my present.

I heard a story once about a guy who was stealing water from his neighbor's well. Well, one day he leaned over too far and fell in. The well was a deep one. It was dark and cold down there; he could barely see the light. He kept yelling and yelling for help. The next day the farmer, who had just come back from market, heard the man yelling from the bottom of the well. The farmer, realizing his neighbor's predicament, and knowing the well was too deep for a ladder, did what he realized was necessary.

The farmer jumped into the well himself. When the neighbor saw this, he was mad…screaming, yelling, angry mad. "What are you doing? Now there is no one to rescue either of us!" The farmer softly spoke, "Don't worry, neighbor, I have been down here in this dark pit before. I know how to get back into the light."

It doesn't matter how deep of a hole I feel that I have dug for myself; it is not too deep for the unlimited abundance of God and the Universe. Become aware. By becoming aware, we will recognize the hand that is being held out to us. All we have to do is grasp it. The hand is being held out by the one who forgives us.

The laws and principles of God and the Universe have been laid out in a clear fashion. Let's follow the Invisible Truth and forgive others and ourselves, and any hole that we have dug is filled up faster.

The power of forgiveness allows the universe to move forward in creating great things. Forgiveness will change the world.

Our subconscious is creating every second, minute and hour of the day. Give our subconscious mind solid materials from our conscious mind to create an outer and inner world with. Forgiveness allows us to live in the now, and not the past. Dwelling on the negative does not manifest one single thing in our present that is beneficial to our future.

An individual who forgives is a happy and peaceful soul. The greater the forgiveness in the individual, the greater the individual's world.

Have forgiveness in our heart and live in peace.

To forgive is the highest, most beautiful form of love. In return, you will receive untold peace and happiness. — Robert Muller

Action Steps for the Week

- Forgive others. Be aware of our anger and thoughts toward people. Change those thoughts immediately to good thoughts. This brings to us the same energy (thoughts, words, beliefs and actions) that we are putting into the world.

- Forgive ourselves, choose to live in the now, and let our mind focus on the good. When we continue to dwell on something that we have done, we manifest that very thing back into our life. Focus on peace and happiness, and good things manifest into our life.

- Confess our sins. Honestly, fully and completely, to ourselves.

- Every time an agonizing memory smacks us down, see it for what it is. See it honestly. Consciously decide to put a positive spin on it. Choose a proactive solution with clear steps. Do these steps to gain a positive attitude instead of wallowing in the mud.

- Ask for forgiveness. Whether that is from our Supreme Being or a friend, acquaintance or business associate, get squared away with our world.

- Let it go. Whatever it is, let it go. "Freedom to, not freedom from."

Law and Principle # 8

Giving and Receiving

*There is a wonderful mythical law of nature that the three things
we crave most in life - happiness, freedom, and peace of mind - are
always attained by giving them to someone else.*
— Peyton Conway March

Giving

By giving, we open the door to receiving. The energy that flows
through the act of giving is a positive energy that acts like a
magnet. We open the door to the universe through our generosity.

The vibrational frequency that flows from giving is immense.
When we add giving to the rest of the laws and principles, we find
that the flow of blessings is magnified. Giving is a key ingredient
to bringing to our lives the abundance we choose to manifest.

We give our time, our effort, our love.

In our job, we give our time. We are actually selling our time and
effort. What we receive for the effort and time we give to our job
has been calculated to have a certain monetary value. We are
compensated at the wage that has been set by the business world
based on the value that consumers are willing to pay for our
service. Bosses don't just pay whatever they wish to pay. There is
a base economy that the market has set for our time and effort.

There is a key word in the above statement. Value. The value we receive (money), is based on what the universe (consumer) is willing to pay for what we give (time and effort). Yes, there are circumstances in which there are differences between what one company pays its people compared to another company, given the same function, within the same economic region. However, the amount paid (received) is hardly ever so wildly different as to be of any real significance. Economics are a (pseudo) science. The energy received (reward) we get from our job is directly proportional to the energy spent, and effort and time that we give towards that job.

I realize that this concept is difficult to swallow for some. There may seem to be an inequity between the time and effort we give compared to the value we receive. There are so many variables here that lead to this sense of inequity that spelling them out is somewhat redundant to the lessons we have already read in this book.

I also understand that many of us give to our community without even realizing we are doing it. It has become so ingrained into our very being that the blessings bestowed upon us are almost a given. This great country of ours is made up of volunteers. Watching the sister's kids so she can go shopping "in peace," coaching a little league baseball team, giving blood, writing a check to the Red Cross, helping a friend move, whatever it is, I know that we have done something. I am always so amazed at the outpouring of efforts from the people of this great world we live in, efforts that go unrewarded, at least to the visible eye.

Giving is also a concept that can be taken to our workplace.

Here are some questions to go through as we think about our job.
- What would I be willing to give for the service I provide?
- What have I done to prepare for the work that I perform?
- How does what I create give value to the world? (How does what I do help create more money in the world? How does what I do better people's lives?)

An example. If I work in a warehouse that supplies metals (as a distributor) to the business world, how does that create value? Well…what have I done to prepare myself for that job? I received my high school diploma. My employer sees that I (should) have a grasp of basic mathematics (measuring, adding and subtracting) in order to perform the work. I am fit to perform the work, as it is a physical job that requires a lot of walking and lifting. I got the job because a friend referred me. Now, though this is a good and honorable job, is it what I have chosen for my inner self, for my own personal happiness?

Taking it a step further, let's look at where the value of my work leads.

The ore that makes the metals I work with comes from the earth and is then sold to the mills. The mills produce the metals and cut them to size. The metals are then transported to the warehouse. The distributor (where we work) then buys the metals and stores them. A manufacturer will then buy the metals from the distributor in order to take the material and machine it into a specific part that they then sell to another company. That company will take the part the manufacturer has produced and install it into a bigger product. That product will go into the finished product. The actual finished product is now a part of a larger product which makes the end product complete. There is a difference between a finished product and the end product.

Let's just say that the metal described here goes into the manufacture of a jet used by an airline. The final consumer is not the airline buying the jet, but the parent who buys his family tickets to fly safely to Disneyland.

There are a multitude of steps throughout all creation, and in every phase of the process there is competition. I am not just talking about the manufacture of physical goods…think about it.

We are each a very valuable and necessary part of the process. Understanding that we help people enjoy their Disneyland vacation is essential in understanding the value we bring to the world.

Appreciating the value we bring to the world further enhances our ability to create at a higher level which, in turn, allows us to give even more of ourselves in a manner that is rewarded at an even higher level.

The point is this. The variables involved in the value received (paycheck) for the time and effort given (work) are many. We are all part of the "machinery" that allows the energy of the universe to flow, change direction and manifest desired results.

The point of Invisible Truth is to understand that we are part of the directional change of the universe's energy and we own the fact that we are not only creating the desired results for others (the owners of the land that the ore is mined, the mill where the metal is produced, the distributor, the manufacturer, the jet builder, the airline…and the little girl who is so excited to go to Disneyland that she can't sleep for a week before the trip), we are also creating our own desired results.

Are we creating our desired results? Do we, yet, understand and realize what our desired results are? Are they clear? Do we have a vision of where we desire to be? This process starts with becoming aware.

I am thankful for the work I do, enjoy the people who I work with, and understand my value to the company. I am receiving what I have given.

Clarifying our place in the work world allows us to understand what we must accomplish to get to the next level on our way to manifesting what we desire.

I am receiving value for what I create. Are we all?

I use these analogies in order to create an understanding of how the laws of attraction work with regard to giving and receiving. The universe brings back to us that which we put forth. Just because we were given a job when we were a kid, were a good employee who never complained, were at work every day and worked very hard does not mean that we will become a millionaire. It means that we are receiving from the work world the value that we are putting in. It is as simple as that.

The universe works the same way. I don't care how smart we think we are; unrewarded genius is almost a proverb. It is when we give to the world our strength, our talent, our gift, that the world gives in return. Whining about it isn't going to get us anywhere. When we are locked into the negative vibration of envy or jealousy about how hard we work to make our boss more money, then that is all we will ever do.

When we have a vision of where we desire to be with our life, and understand that our current job is a means to an end in realizing our vision, then we free ourselves of the murky water filling our bucket and begin to attract the positive energy of the universe that accelerates our realizing (manifesting) our vision.

The value that we give to the world is directly related to the value we receive.

Most of the time direct correlations are elusive. However, changing the direction of that which we receive to further our path toward our desired result is the key. Having faith that the world gives back is part of the process. Sometimes what we receive is not anything that we would think that we desire. However, there is a lesson to be learned in that situation that has presented itself to us which we must work through in order to manifest our desired result.

Taking responsibility for that which has been "laid before us" and controlling the next step in the chain of "cause and effect" allows us to control the future in a positive way, no matter the circumstance before us.

By taking responsibility (being aware) for the cause and taking control of variables within the result, we become the catalyst of the next chain of events that stem from the original "cause." We can change the flow of energy from negative to positive...or change the energy from positive to even more positive. The choice is ours.

Keep the vision. Keep moving forward with integrity and trust. Success is to just keep going in the right direction.

It is every man's obligation to put back into the world at least the equivalent of what he takes out of it. — Albert Einstein

The Well Known Garden Analogy

I desire to grow vegetables in my garden. This isn't done by going outside in the backyard and throwing out some seed. First, I must prepare the garden bed to receive the seed. Once I plant the seed, I will tend my garden by watering, weeding and nurturing the plants. Prior to the growing season, I do some research and find out there is this special, steer fertilizer from Argentina, from cattle that have been fed no chemicals nor hormones, is completely organic, and is supposed to grow huge crops when used as a fertilizer. I track it down and use it in my garden.

I give of my time and effort in order to manifest that which I desire, great, big, healthy, organic vegetables. My crop ripens into a bountiful harvest. So bountiful, in fact, that I give away much of what I have grown to those who appreciate it. I also get the bonus of more seed for next season's garden, which I have, again, prepared the earth for.

I have put in the work (given), received the bounty, and have shared my bounty (given). The energy that I have given to the universe returns to me in ways I may never recognize. I believe it to be true, and I have faith that I am receiving my reward.

I gave before I received. What I received was abundance, which in turn I gave again.

It all starts with giving.

Giving is better than receiving because giving starts the receiving process. — Jim Rohn

Here is the cyclical nature of giving. The more we give, the more we are given to give, the more we receive. It is a continuous cycle of giving and receiving which continues as long as we are giving.

Proverbs 22:9 A generous man will himself be blessed, for he shares his food with the poor. (NIV)

My Vision and My Plan

Create our vision. Give to the universe as we do the work to realize our vision. The universe responds in ways unimaginable.

I have created dozens of business plans for companies I have been involved with at some level. However, until recently, I did not have a "business plan" for my life. I had no mission statement, no goals, no objectives, no strategy…and therefore, nothing to implement because I had no life vision.

I give to the world because it is my nature…but what I have received, though good, has been random and not specific.

Since I began the research on the Invisible Truth, I have changed that. I have created my mission statement, which helped develop my vision. My mission statement started with a vague vision which was not too specific. As I wrote my mission, I put my vision into words.

This took me months of writing, and rewriting, in order to create six sentences. I now own my mission and, at the same time, realize that it is flexible and can change as circumstances change. However, the first line will never change. "I choose to be a positive force in the universe." My mission statement is centered around what it is that I wish to give to the world to make it a better place.

I then set my goals. They are lofty. They are big. Why not? They are my goals and I can make them whatever I desire. I have written the things I choose to receive from the universe. I chose goals that, once achieved, will allow me to further my mission in a very significant way. They will change the world.

I have set my objectives. I have created benchmarks by which I know that I have achieved specific goals.

I have set my strategy. I have set specific steps of how I will achieve my goals and objectives. They outline what, specifically, I choose to produce to give to the world and what, specifically, I choose to receive from the world. The value I receive from what I choose to give to the world through my work product is only a portion of my strategy. By itself, it will be insufficient to fulfill my vision.

Therefore, I have set within my strategy ways that I choose to get to my goals and objectives that are outside of the monetary value I receive from my job. Some of these strategies have to do with further education, creating outside income, and volunteering in the community. All of my strategies are based on creating positive energy in the universe.

I have created a plan for the implementation of specific things I will achieve in order to further my strategy. As an example, I know exactly how I choose to create my income, how I choose to supplement my income, what, exactly, I require to educate myself on in order to further and increase my income, and specifically what it is that I choose to do to give back to the community in a way that I enjoy.

In other words, I volunteer for the very selfish reason that I enjoy it. It gives me great satisfaction to do the things I do in this world, which is a reward in and of itself. What the universe brings to me, in return, is a bonus.

Create the plan. It starts with giving. With me, the deal is, I desire to give at a much higher value rate. Therefore, I have a plan. I choose to change the universe in a big way, and I know how.

We make a living by what we get, but we make a life by what we give. — Winston Churchill

The Challenge

A problem will develop when one violates the divine laws or principles of God or the dynamics of nature. On occasion, our lives hit blocks. We lose our job, or a loved one dies, or our house is flooded. Whatever the challenge is, when we stop giving to others or to the world, the dirty hose gets turned back on.

If we allow ourselves to become the victim again, the dirty hose gets turned up to full blast. The words that we most wish to avoid come back into our lives. Fear, lack, want. At that point the giving is shut off, which, in turn, turns off the receiving. It is a bit of a vicious circle.

There is always a way to give back, no matter how small. If nothing else, there is giving thanks for our life. The power of giving is not to be underestimated. Giving is like putting money in the bank. The return is compounded with interest.

Giving is energy of such a high frequency vibration that life itself is created. Conception is giving. Bringing a life into the world is giving of the highest magnitude. When giving is connected with love and belief, the power of the return is magnified dynamically.

I look at my children and know that I have given all that I could to them in the best way I knew how. The return I receive is immeasurable. Just a smile and a laugh is enough for me, but I receive so much more, it is always a wonder to me…and I give thanks.

We can give of ourselves, our time, our knowledge, or whatever it is that we have to give. We can also give of our finances, the fruits of our labor.

Proverbs 3:9-10 Honor the Lord with your wealth, with the first fruits of all your crops; then your barns will be filled to overflowing, and your vats will brim over with new wine. (NIV)

Give from the first fruits of our labor and our barns are filled with plenty. We do receive.

Hand out a smile on our way out of the building or house today. Watch what happens. I'll bet that if there is more than one person in the room they'll all smile. Giving gets contagious after awhile. When we give of our knowledge, we gain more than what we gave. What knowledge we gave we already knew, and if we learn one thing that adds to our knowledge, then the effort of giving our knowledge has paid off in ways that we may not understand at the time. When we give love, in abundance, love is returned to us...in abundance.

The love we give away is the only love we keep. — Elbert Hubbard

When we give, the door opens for us to receive in abundance. When we give, give with a cheerful heart.

2 Corinthians 9:7 Each man should give what he has decided in his heart to give, not reluctantly or under compulsion, for God loves a cheerful giver. (NIV)

When we give begrudgingly, we diminish the blessing because our energy is low. Low vibration attracts low vibrating things to us. We are negating the purpose of giving. When we are a cheerful giver, we are sending out vibrations of a higher magnitude. And we are attracting things into our lives of the same or greater magnitude.

2 Corinthians 9:6 Remember this: Whoever sows sparingly will also reap sparingly, and whoever sows generously will also reap generously. (NIV)

When we think, speak and believe bountifully, we are sowing bountifully. When we work, are thankful, and forgive, we are sowing bountifully.

Following the Invisible Truth is sowing bountifully. And what we sow, we shall reap. It is our choice. The Universe is unlimited and can deliver abundance with great ease. It is our limited mind that limits abundance.

Dream Big; Receive Big

The Universe is in constant creation and expansion. Change is happening moment by moment. The changes in our lives are continuous.

When I sew all of these laws and principles together, I perceive the forces of nature and the divine power of my Supreme Being as more in my favor.

I choose to use scripture because it allows me to give analogies and concepts that bring forth greater understanding of how the laws and principles work in my life. These concepts are true in most major religions and philosophies worldwide.

In giving, it is not how much we give that is bountiful sowing; it is how much we give of what we are able to give that is bountiful sowing. It is where our heart is at when it comes to giving.

2 Corinthians 8:12 For if the willingness is there, the gift is acceptable according to what one has, not according to what he does not have. (NIV)

Bountiful sowing is cheerful giving no matter who we are, rich or poor.

2 Corinthians 9:10 Now he who supplies seed to the sower and bread for food will also supply and increase your store of seed and will enlarge the harvest of your righteousness. (NIV)

Cheerful giving is planting our seed. When we plant our seed, we begin the sowing process. When we sew the nine laws and principles together then we reap the ability for unlimited abundance in our life.

The principle of giving goes hand in hand with that of receiving. There are those who give and receive…then there are those who are takers only. Those who give receive in abundance. Those who are only takers create lack in their lives. Understand those who do nothing but take.

To give from our garden is to follow the laws of nature. When we couple the rest of the laws and principles with cheerful giving, we see a tree of abundance grow before our eyes.

Have faith and believe in the power of giving. Give of our increase cheerfully, and watch our barns get filled with abundance.

When I give, I give gladly. If the person or organization I give to squanders the money, I have learned something. (Fool me once…!) If the person or organization I give to uses my gift in a good way, I am happy…and I have learned something.

Be wise in our giving and give happily. Give, do not loan…unless we are performing a business transaction. When we give, do so with a happy heart and with no expectations. If we expect a return on what we give, it won't happen, or we could be disappointed. These are negative vibrations which create lack and want. If we give freely, and it comes back to us, think of how joyful we are to receive that which we did not expect.

If a buddy is a little short this week and asks to borrow 50 dollars, and it is within our ability to give him or her money, do so without qualms, reservation or agenda. Just give them the money. If they squander it on booze, we will have learned a valuable (and expensive) lesson…and won't do it again.

If they use it as part of their rent payment, then our reward is that we helped keep them sheltered. If they pay us back as soon as they can, we are joyful and have also learned a valuable lesson about this person. (Was it worth 50 dollars to find that out?) We have also created a situation where, should we ever be a little short, and that friend has extra funds….

A cheerful giver is a happy soul.

Be honest. Be respectful. Have integrity. Give. Let God out.

Just as importantly, but not part of the subject here, is to be a good steward of the money that is given to us. A good steward is blessed with more abundance.

Directed, Controlled, Organized Energy

A river is energy in motion. Another word for that would be current. Just as the movement of electricity through a wire is an electrical current, the movement of air or wind in the same direction is a current.

These currents are the movement of energy. The swifter the currents are, the more power that is generated.

Money is currency, or a current. The movement of money is energy. Power is generated when this current, this energy, is flowing. It's a current of currency flowing abundantly in my life.

The stronger the current of the river, electricity or wind (or money) is, the more power that is generated. When we give our money, our time, our knowledge or whatever it is that we choose to give, a flow, or current, of energy is happening.

The more of these laws and principles that are working harmoniously together, the stronger the current becomes, the more power that is generated. The more power that is generated, the faster our desired reality is created.

We all have uncontrolled, disorganized energy which is random and compulsive. We also have directed, controlled, organized energy which is called awareness, consciousness and choice.

We are now able to choose what we fill our bucket with to overflow our desired reality into our life.

Things naturally move toward disorganized energy. To keep a system of positive motion, choose a directed flow of organized energy.

When we have directed, organized energy in the form of these conscious laws and principles working synergistically together, the current is strong and the power of abundance is magnified.

Receiving

Receiving is the other half of giving. We will receive. It is okay to receive. The more that we receive, the more that we have to give. Nature is set up for us to receive, as long as we are giving. The divine writings and philosophies from thousands of years ago state this very thing.

Here in America, the majority of people enter into retirement age with far less than is required to live in the manner they were used to while they were working. Part of the reason is the culture that was created around the thought that "money is the root of all evil." Well, I don't know where that came from because it certainly didn't come from God.

I actually know people who have stated to me "I hate money." Well, guess what, they don't have any. They complain about not having any, and, out of the other side of their mouth, tell me they hate money.

The shame is that we pass this same system on to our children. Our children have been programmed from an early age to stop the money flow. I call this the money dam. It is a dam that blocks the current of money from flowing to them. People have been taught that receiving in abundance is bad.

These dams become generational challenges until someone decides to tear them down. That someone could be us. Are we going to choose to create generations of abundance from now on?

The puritan, Anglo world of North America is vested in the tyrannical teachings of Bible thumpers of another age who were flat out wrong. Regarding money, we have been taught, in spoken and unspoken words, that we would be in jeopardy of committing three, maybe four, of the seven Cardinal sins if we had too much money. Greed, gluttony, envy and pride. Hogwash. A sinner is a sinner, regardless of the amount of money they have. Thank goodness Getty, Rockefeller, Ford, Gates and so many others weren't listening.

Throughout the teachings of Invisible Truth, we have learned laws and principles to set us on our corrected way.

Money

With the Invisible Truth, we are learning the method to open our lives to abundance, whether it is of wealth, health or spiritual enlightenment. We are learning to turn the flow of duplicative power up high.

We are learning how to eliminate the patterns of self-sabotage in our lives, and how to get rid of our money dams. By retraining the way we think about creating our vision and working toward our vision, we are giving the magic of the universe by creating abundance to our comfort level.

After working with many people while developing Invisible Truth, I have found a reoccurring theme for money dams in their lives.

Most people have been programmed to associate wealth and prosperity with unethical and evil ways (more of that puritan stuff).

The underlying belief is that it is wrong or unethical to have wealth and prosperity. This is just not true. Now, understand that wealth and prosperity is defined by each individual at their own level of comfort and desire. Only one of the "measurements" of wealth and prosperity is money. With regards to money and wealth, prosperity is only defined as financial freedom...freedom to live at the level with which we are comfortable.

A simple soul who lives a simple life and who has no desire to drive a Porsche, live in a big house on a golf course, and be surrounded with material things, does not have the same requirements for wealth as the mansion owner. There is nothing wrong with living a simple life, nor is there anything wrong with desire for the Porsche, big house, etc. The only difference is the financial freedom required to maintain the desired lifestyle.

Financial freedom is nothing more than the goal one must achieve in order to fulfill their mission statement. If our mission statement begins and ends with the acquisition and hording of money and "things," then we had better look at our priorities again...because we have missed the boat...and will die alone with our money and "things."

Luke 12:31 But seek his kingdom, and these things will be given to you as well. (NIV)

Seeking the kingdom of God means giving ourselves over to the principles of good, the principles of right...and following the laws and principles that have been set forth in the divine writings that each of us chooses to follow.

Whatever our choice of beliefs, they follow the same laws and principles of Nature and the Universe.

Some of the most "Christian" people I know profess to believe in God or Christianity or Buddhism or one of many other faiths. They are good, kind and clean souls. We have all seen the inequities of those who profess to be servants of God, and then have seen them sin with their actions. Many of the sins were around money.

Understand this: money is nothing more than a tool. It is a tool that can be used for good, or for evil. The creation of money is not a sin, in and of itself. Like everything else, it is what we do with that which comes to us that might be a sin.

Once we take away the emotion wrapped around the concept of money, we begin to see it as nothing more than a tool. It is just another tool to get us where we wish to be.

If the creation of money is the end all for us, we have missed the point anyway. Money is not evil; creating money solely for the sake of owning it is evil. Money is a consequence of creation, and when used for betterment gives back to the world.

We are seeking the kingdom of God when we follow the ways of God and the laws of the Universe. Incorporate the laws and principles with whatever our faith is first and anything is possible.

It has been shown scientifically that directed, controlled, organized energy is powerful in the manifestation of our outer and inner worlds.

It is okay to receive. When we give, allow ourselves to receive, and count all that we receive as a blessing. Use the abundance we have received to do good, and that, in turn, brings to us abundance that we can use for more good.

Proverbs 10:22 The blessing of the Lord brings wealth, and he adds no trouble to it. (NIV)

Can it get any clearer than this? God adds no trouble to wealth. Well…it must be us and all of the emotions we have wrapped around money that brings trouble to it.

Many a clergyman has professed that the meaning of this statement was to be interpreted with "wealth in the kingdom of God." Why? Could it be that the interpretations of those who have been responsible for the teachings of the scripture were wrong? Throughout the Bible, I have found nothing telling me that having money is wrong. However, there is plenty to say about doing evil with money, or making money "my God." So, it gets back to doing the right thing.

Psalms 35:27 May those who delight in my vindication shout for joy and gladness; may they always say, "The Lord be exalted, who delights in the well-being of his servant." (NIV)

God desires for us to do well, and when we do, He and the universe are provided with good and positive energy.

Do we think for a moment that our God, or Supreme Being, or the Universe, find anything positive in our failure? Do we think that our failure is buying us any juice in the hereafter?

Following the Invisible Truth brings us wealth (however we define that), and the Lord...as well as the Universe, is happy with that.

It is when we don't follow the laws and principles that we get into trouble. That is when our dirty hose goes on full blast.

Proverbs 15:27 A greedy man brings trouble to his family, but he who hates bribes will live. (NIV)

Earth provides enough for every man's need, but not every man's greed. — Mahatma Gandhi

When an individual has forgotten that the Universe, or their God, has unlimited abundance, and they lie, cheat and steal to get ahead, they are the individuals who run into the problems.

Greed is the bottomless pit which exhausts the person in an endless effort to satisfy the need without ever reaching satisfaction — Erich Fromm

People who focus on debt, who continuously want, who believe it is a dog-eat-dog world, are those who either choose not to understand, or choose to ignore that there is unlimited abundance in the universe. God says so, and that is good enough for me. However, the laws of the universe say so too.

Those who feel greed will never find peace.

There are some who seek riches because they believe that with riches comes happiness. Seeking riches for riches' sake is an empty dream, and with it comes an unfulfilled destiny.

Synopsis

We control the past and the future by living in the present moment. Our thoughts control the words we say. We become the words we say and, thereby, adjust the thoughts we have. Our belief comes in line with our thoughts and words.

We are, continuously and for the rest of our lives, aware of the words we say, the thoughts we have, and what we believe. We are disciplined in our vigilance of our awareness of these thoughts, words and beliefs. In so doing, we are working toward the vision we have created and have written down as our mission.

As we work towards our vision, we are carrying the conviction of our beliefs to their conclusion, being thankful for all that we have. As we give thanks for the blessings in our lives, we also are giving thanks for our ability to forgive those who have done us wrong, and to seek forgiveness from those we have wronged, while forgiving ourselves along the way.

As our abundance increases, we are not forgetting to give to those who require a step up, a little help in their life to get them going. Though we give of ourselves and our money freely and with no expectations, we pay attention to what is done with the money so that we will not be played a fool in its use. Even more valuable than our giving money is our giving of our time. Money can always be reproduced; time cannot. We understand that through giving we are opening the doors to the abundance of the universe.

Action Steps for the Week

- Continue our discipline of awareness.

- Start to create our life plan. Make it colossal. Examine our vision. Make it stupendous. Understand that though our plan is flexible, our personal statement of our ultimate mission is not. (That first sentence in our mission statement is where we place our ultimate mission.)

- We will create a life plan which is a pyramid built of the following, with each step becoming more specific in detail: our mission statement, goals, objectives, strategy and implementation plans. This exercise will help create our vision which, in turn, will help create our mission.

- Give of ourselves to those around us. Give our time, our love, our money. Volunteer at a rest home, coach a team, be a student tutor, help in a classroom, run a scout troop, work at the food bank, write a check to the Red Cross, go give blood...come on, do something. Pay it forward.

- Examine what our thoughts are about money, how it makes us feel, what we think about it. If it is a block, work to unblock it, remembering that money is nothing more than a tool.

- Give a portion of our increase to a charity or someone who is making a difference in the world.

- Donate some of our time to help or benefit someone else.

- Be aware and conscious that receiving in abundance is the other half of giving.

Law and Principle # 9

Our Environment

Our environment, the world in which we live and work, is a mirror of our attitudes and expectations. — Earl Nightingale

Cleansing our environment is necessary for our intuition and guidance to become clear. Cleansing our environment is about clearing the distractions in our path. A clean environment gives us the ability to forge peace within the other laws and principles.

Cleaning up my environment physically, spiritually, intellectually and emotionally to the degree that is right for me...ever seen a picture of Einstein's office? It was right for him.

How we present ourselves is a direct reflection of how we see ourselves.

Given any circumstance, my environment is a direct reflection of my view of my own self, my spirit and my soul. I have control. I may not have full control of the circumstance, but as we have learned, I have control of my reaction and creation, given any circumstance.

I also have control of my re-creation. If the circumstance is good, I can re-create it. If my circumstance is bad, I have control over not allowing it to be re-created.

Creating harmoniously with these laws and principles is about controlling our environment. It is about how we react to our environment and how our environment reacts to us.

How I react to the circumstance that surrounds me helps dictate my environment moving forward. I control my environment. My environment does not control me.

You are a product of your environment. So choose the environment that will best develop you toward your objective. Analyze your life in terms of its environment. Are the things around you helping you toward success - or are they holding you back?
— W. Clement Stone

Just as we should cultivate gentle and peaceful relations with our fellow human beings, we should also extend that same kind of attitude towards the natural environment. Morally speaking, we should be concerned for our whole environment.
— Dalai Lama

Our Space

The space I live in, both at work and at home, is a direct reflection of the energy I choose to put into the world. I take responsibility for that. I own that. The space I live in is not necessarily the things I surround myself with. It is the love and energy I put into that space.

How many times have we been in a home or building that, though beautiful to look at, had no soul? The space felt desolate. I have made the conscious decision to fill the space I live in with the energy I choose to surround myself with. I choose to surround myself with good, clean energy. What do we choose?

I understand that the energy I put into the space I live in is reflected back at me in like kind. I also understand that circumstance will influence my choice. It is tough to have a 1,000 dollar dream on a 100 dollar budget. Maintain that 1,000 dollar dream. Find comfort and satisfaction in our 100 dollar budget while striving for the 1,000 dollar dream.

Look around. What are the colors of the energy we surround ourselves with?

The People in Our Lives

People who have a direct and immediate impact in our personal lives. Family, friends and close associates have some control over our environment. Because of our relationship with that person, or these people, we have given them some power in our lives. Beyond childhood, the amount of control we give to another is by choice. If that person, or those people, are harming me, whose responsibility is it?

The things we hear and see make up a great deal of what we communicate. When we surround ourselves with pessimistic people, with doom-and-gloomers, guess what we are going to be talking about?

We have become aware of the consequences of allowing unfiltered garbage to run into our heads from other people. We have decided to keep and maintain our own power, and not give it to others. We have decided that their reality is not necessarily ours.

If I surround myself with the movers and shakers who charge through life with a positive force, I feel better. I move forward emulating their actions. The results of these actions continually reinforce the positive, life altering patterns of a healthy mind. A healthy mind strives to find the answer, whether it be God's answer, the universe's answer, or our answer. As the old adage goes, "it is the journey, not the destination." Enjoy the journey. We hold our truth while being aware that there is a real truth and we are striving to realize it.

We continue to look for the right questions.

To put the world right in order, we must first put the nation in order; to put the nation in order, we must first put the family in order; to put the family in order, we must first cultivate our personal life; we must first set our hearts right.
— Confucius

The People Outside Our Lives

To a lesser degree, we are influenced by those who live outside our direct environment. The environments we have less control over includes the workplace, the grocery store and the highway.

In this environment, the most intimate influence comes from the workplace. At least 20 to 24 percent of our time is spent with people who have a direct influence on our lives, but not necessarily our personal environment. How, and to what extent, we choose to allow these people to directly influence our environment is strictly up to us. Do we take our work home?

There are people saying things every day that affect us in ways we have, until now, had no idea of the impact on us. How did this news around the water cooler affect us? Did it give us positive energy? Did it drain us? Are we even aware how it affected us?

More importantly, if we carry our work home with us, are we choosing to do so? Given the circumstance, did we give it our best effort? Are we able to release the situation at the end of the day? If we have given our best, let it go.

Take Control

The massive onslaught of information coming at us throughout our day is so pervasive that unless we are aware and control its intake it controls how we think, speak and behave.

The point is...take control. We have the choice. We are aware. If we choose to read the newspaper, watch the news on TV, read the blogs online...do it with awareness. The world will make us sick...if we allow it to happen.

Understand that the TV we are watching is designed to "tell a vision." Ask ourselves if the vision we are absorbing is one we feel positive about. Is it something we choose to have in our subconscious when we fall asleep? Food for thought.

I choose to be aware of what is happening in the world. I have chosen to get the majority of my news online. It allows me the ability to "click into" the news I choose to read. I am also aware of what it is that I am absorbing and how it affects my life, what it makes me think, and how it makes me feel. By looking at my thoughts from a somewhat objective standpoint, it allows me to control my judgments of what it is that I am looking at, which, in turn, allows me to choose how I feel about a subject.

I have taken control.

Food

Mother Earth gave us everything we need in order to live long healthy lives. Notice I have used "need" in this sentence? Food is, obviously, a need in our lives.

Let food be your medicine and medicine be your food.
— Hippocrates

Mother Earth also gave us all of the natural elements with which to heal ourselves when we are sick. Whether we take natural supplements, naturopathic remedies or prescribed medicines, all have an original base in something Mother Earth has provided.

If drugs were the answer, we'd be the healthiest people on the planet. — Dr. Mark McClellan, Administrator of Medicare and Medicaid Services.

Over the generations, technology has advanced to the point where food production has become a science. It is abundant, and it is relatively inexpensive. Life spans have increased dramatically over the last century, and much of that can be attributed to the quality and quantity of food that is available to us now. But, it has come at a cost. At this point in the evolution of humanity, we are beginning to poison ourselves.

Technology has led to the harvest of crops on such massive scales that it has sucked the nutrients out of the soil, leaving the foods that come from the earth so depleted of the nutrients that our bodies naturally hunger for that we are eating huge amounts of

food to attempt to feel like we are getting what we require to
survive. Many people are stuffed, yet starving.

We never know the worth of water till the well is dry.
— Thomas Fuller

The Toxic Outside

*I think the environment should be put in the category of our
national security. Defense of our resources is just as important as
defense abroad. Otherwise what is there to defend?*
— Robert Redford

This leads to another type of physical environment. The physical
world around us. The toxins that have been created through the
industrialization and urbanization of the world are negatively
affecting all living beings. The heavy metal contaminants alone are
so insidious in any urban area that with every breathe we take we
are inhaling a poison of some form into our bodies. We can
counteract this.

Understanding the world we live in, I have chosen to give my body
the best possible opportunity to fight off the poisons that the world
produces. The human body is the most amazing, and the least
understood, machine ever created. If I feed it the right foods, and
consciously supplement my diet with the natural elements that are
lacking in the foods I eat, I am boosting my immune system to
fight off disease in a way that medicine cannot. The food I eat is
considered before I consume it. The supplements I take are
purposeful, specific and studied. They are natural and can be
categorized as food. They are not chemical versions of vitamins;
they are more aptly named carefully dehydrated food.

*The doctor of the future will give no medicine but will interest his
patients in the care of the human frame, in diet and the cause and
prevention of disease.* — Thomas Edison

It comes back to the bucket. The toxins I had unconsciously put into my body are being flushed out through a very conscious effort on my part.

What if

What if I put the newspaper down, turned off the news, skipped the onslaught from the internet, ignored the blogs, didn't use my cell for anything other than phone calls, and what if I actually engaged in live conversations with others?

My immediate reaction is…I would no longer have to live with the ups and downs of the baseball teams I follow. No, I am not going that far…but, they do make me crazy. I can, however, consciously filter the rest of it.

What do we suppose would happen if we chose to unplug? How about at least at the end of the work day? Would the world end? Goodness, some people can't even unplug enough to read a book.

When was the last time we went out at night, laid on our back and stared up at the stars?

What would happen if we went home and there were no electronic communication devices available? No phone, TV, iPod, computer, Xbox…nothing. What would happen if we actually talked to our spouse, mate, kids, parents, neighbors?

Just imagine the look on our spouse's face or the kids' faces if we walked in and turned everything off and told them we were calling for a family discussion. The first question they are going to ask is "What's wrong?"

Would the world end if we stopped for an hour (a day, a week…a month) and enjoyed the reason we are here on this spectacular planet? If we still don't know why we are here, time to go back to the beginning of the book. I will be here when you return.

To see what is right, and not to do it, is want of courage or of principle. — Confucius

We are in control. We control our thoughts, words and what we believe. We work toward our destiny each day. We're thankful for all the blessings bestowed upon us, and we forgive ourselves and others. We give all that we choose in a way that brings us pleasure. We control our environment.

You see, it's never the environment; it's never the events of our lives, but the meaning we attach to the events - how we interpret them - that shapes who we are today and who we'll become tomorrow. — Tony Robbins

Hebrews 10:22 Let us draw near to God with a sincere heart and with the full assurance that faith brings, having our hearts sprinkled to cleanse us from a guilty conscience and having our bodies washed with pure water. (NIV)

Action Steps for the Week

- Become aware of our space. Does it reflect how we choose to see ourselves?

- Become aware of how we feel and respond to the people who have a direct effect on our life and all that entails.

- Become aware of how we feel and respond to the people who have an indirect effect on our life. These include workmates or people we deal with on a daily basis in the normal course of our life. Be aware of the effect they cause, as well as the effect we have on them.

- Study the food we eat. Is it good for us?

- Become aware of the changes we desire. Decisively make the changes while not offending. Allow for our world to align in the direction that most brings us peace.

Putting It All Together

How to Cause the Laws of Attraction to Work for Us

If the creation of your life does not provide the emotion you desire,
then change your creation. — Will A. Rainmaker

How's it working for you so far? Your life, that is?

These laws and principles allow us to harmoniously control the movement of energy in a direction we desire.

We control our lives; our lives do not control us.

To get to where we desire, it is important to remember that it won't happen overnight. The process involves a lifelong dedication and discipline that will, eventually, get us to the place "fate" takes us. The point is that we have control over our "fate."

The universe is creating happenings in our lives with the materials that we are giving it to create with. We attract to us things that vibrate at the same, or greater, level and magnitude of vibration that we are releasing into the universe.

That is why when we choose to follow all nine laws and principles together, these laws and principles work synergistically to cause a much higher energy frequency to be released into the universe. We control what energy we release into the universe.

The universe takes what we have put into it and creates something for us of the same, or greater, magnitude.

It is critical that all nine laws and principles be used in conjunction with each other in order to synergistically flow with the energy of the universe. In so doing, we gain control over the direction of the "cause and effect" in our world.

Following a few of the laws and principles will result in some good, but to get to our intended destiny, all nine must be used in concert.

Move forward, move toward our enlightenment.

1 Corinthians 16:13 Be on your guard; stand firm in the faith; be men of courage; be strong. (NIV)

Accountability

Take responsibility for our life.

We are the one who has created our life, no one else. No matter where we are at, we did it.

When we own this statement, we have cleared the first hurdle to creating what we desire. When we take responsibility for all that has happened in our life, we get rid of the "victim."

Taking responsibility means realizing that the things that have "happened" to us in our life are a direct, or indirect, result of the subconscious energy we have put into the universe.

Yes, there are events in our lives that we have little or no control over. These are, typically, life events that are sudden and random.

However, understanding the event clearly for what it is, and reacting in a way that causes the direction of energy to change into a direction we desire, given the circumstance, allows us to become responsible and accountable. These are events that are "no one's fault," but are life altering. We may not "own" the original cause, but we certainly are responsible for our reaction and subsequent actions. We then take control of the events as they unfold in our world.

That is called taking responsibility.

For all other events in our life, take full responsibility. Remove ourselves from the "blame game." Point our finger directly at our own nose and realize that we have created, exactly, the world we live in.

When we do this, we have taken the first step in taking control of our world and not letting the world control us.

We have begun the process of becoming aware. We are becoming conscious. By becoming conscious, we have started the process of clearing our subconscious of the mud that has accumulated throughout our life.

We are now responsible for all that has ever happened, and all that will ever happen in our life. Accountability allows us to clearly take control of the present moment, the "now," and our lives will forevermore be changed.

By taking responsibility for our lives we become conscious and aware of the moment we live in. We become more aware of the thoughts we have, the words we use and the beliefs we profess. The work we do becomes a conscious, responsible effort towards that which we desire.

By taking responsibility for our lives we naturally become grateful for that which we have, that which we have created, and that which we are creating.

We are doing it. No one else.

When we are accountable for all that we have created, forgiveness is a natural evolution. When we realize that all that has ever happened to us we have allowed to happen, it is only natural to allow forgiveness. To not forgive others means we do not forgive ourselves (for letting that which must be forgiven to happen either through action or through omission). Conversely, by taking responsibility and forgiving others, we forgive ourselves as well.

By taking responsibility and being accountable, we learn humility. Being humble means understanding that we do not create the energy of the universe; we are not God. However, humility allows us to understand the flow of the universe and our part in the control of the direction of energy.

Humility also allows us to understand the change of energy in the universe through our gifts to the universe. By giving of our time, our effort, our money, we put into the universe a positive force that will not be denied. The laws of attraction dictate that whatever energy we give to the universe compounds itself and comes back to us.

Taking responsibility for our lives means understanding that whatever comes back to us is a gift we have received and we are thankful for it. We are responsible for what we gave to the universe; therefore, we are responsible for what we receive.

Taking responsibility also means being in control of our environment. Controlling our environment means analyzing everything that we allow into our world; it means understanding that what we allow into our world influences our flow of energy. Be responsible for the input of clutter the world is bombarding us with. Reject that which is not useful or of no consequence, unless we consciously decide that we wish to engage in whatever the world is bringing to us at any given moment.

Understand that should we choose to engage in information that is being presented we are now filtering it through a (new) system that allows us to use the information in a positive way.

Allowing Our Bucket to Clear Itself

I cannot say this enough. Just because we have started to use the laws of the universe in our favor, it does not mean that peace and prosperity are an overnight result. The journey is lifelong. The end result will be the same for all of us.

The difference is…the journey.

Each of us has our own path in this life. Understanding that we are in control of that path is the way through which we create an evolutionary process of expanding our energy that vibrates in a positive way once we leave the trappings of our current vessel. Along the way we create results in our current life that are what we desire.

Because each of our paths are different, we each have varying amounts of dirt in our buckets. I'd venture to guess that those who are reading this are striving for clarity. There are those whose lives are so filled with mud that they don't even know that there is an alternative…and don't want to know. (See that word *want* in there?) However, these are the individuals who require this work the most. We have some people in our life who are like this. As we proceed through our journey through enlightenment, we will be a good influence on them, and when it is time, we will be there to introduce them to the tools we have used to become more enlightened.

It starts with us.

This journey begins with becoming, and remaining, aware. Become aware of where we are at in our life, and how we view where we are. Sometimes even this is a bit of a stretch. However, we are now aware that we are not quite fully cognizant of where we are at in our life. This, in and of itself, is an excellent start.

Maintaining that awareness, things begin to sift through the new filter system we have created, and our world begins to shift towards that which we desire.

We are conscious of the thoughts we have and the words we use because we are now aware of them. We have begun the process of cleansing the subconscious of all the mud that has flowed into it since the beginning of our life. In so doing, we are now aware of some of the "blocks" that have been created through our observation of the world, the judgments we have placed on these events and the emotions we have wrapped around those judgments.

Remember, it is enough to know that these blocks exist. It is enough to know that we are conscious of them and have chosen to, while acknowledging them, move past them.

They are no longer "blocks."

As we become aware of the thoughts and words that we use, we are filling our subconscious with positive words and thoughts, and we are moving the dirt that has been in our bucket out. Because the outside of our bucket is our conscious world, this is what we see. In other words, this is the time when people quit…no matter what it is that they are learning.

Think about that.

The physics of the matter are this. As we fill a bucket that has dirt in it with pristine water, that dirt flows to the outside. In the analogies we have used here, the outside of the bucket is our conscious mind, the part we are aware of.

This is when people quit. They put into their lives affirmation, positive thinking…whatever their latest training is, and their perceived result (that which is flowing out) is more of the same stuff that was in their lives in the first place…so they quit. All learning is like this.

All of it.

However, this isn't school. There is no greater fear looming over the horizon regarding "if I don't learn this stuff and pass my class.' There is no fear of our parent's wrath if we don't get the grade. There is no fear of not getting the job if I don't pass the course. This is just me desiring to better myself…so when I see the stuff that is coming out of my bucket when I do what is being requested in the learning, I panic…and then quit.

In the world of health and wellbeing, there is a common phrase that is used amongst practitioners. It is called the "healing crisis."

In the naturopathic world it is quite common. When a remedy is suggested and taken, there is often a panic because the symptoms appear to get worse. What is actually happening is that whatever malady is being treated begins to work its way out of the cellular structure of the body and actually make the person feel worse.

This is not the time to quit.

The malady is working itself out of the body and wellness includes being rid of the cause of the illness altogether. The treatment is not a masking of the symptoms, and therefore may cause some discomfort. But, as the cause of the illness leaves the body, we are in a better situation than we would have been by having just added a "painkiller" to mask the symptoms.

It is the same with striving for enlightenment.

There is a "healing crisis" that we all go through. The questions…the doubts…more self-judgment because we are not "perfect" after the first time through.

Visualize where we desire to be in our emotional life. Hold that vision. Keep working through the process until it is no longer a struggle to do the work. It becomes a pleasure.

Doing the work opens "Pandora's box." All that stuff we have suppressed for years comes to the surface. Recognize it. Acknowledge it. Move on. Most of us are willing and ready to do this…we just require a little direction.

Some of us are not even aware of our Pandora's box. Pandora was a character from Greek mythology. The box she was given contained all the evils of the world. She was told not to open it.

Well, we know what happened, she opened it anyway. All the evils of the world were released (hate, anger, sickness, greed, vanity, etc.). When she slammed the lid back on, all that was left in the box was hope.

Hope, being trapped in the box, was construed as one of the world's evils. However, it also has been thought of as the one dream of man that has kept the world in balance. As stated previously, hope, by itself, is a toothless emotion that leads to ruin.

The opposite of hope is hopelessness. Hope as a word of action and work is a powerful manifestation of good.

We just know that there are portions of our life that we do not wish to confront. This our own Pandora's box.

Some of us have held the box in our hands and viewed its contents. Some of us have slammed the lid shut and put it to the side. Some of us are aware that we have it, but keep it locked in a closet. Every now and then we open the closet and see it, get what we came for, and quickly shut the door again. Some of us won't even approach the room that has the closet holding the box. Some of us avoid that part of the house altogether. Some of us move to another state and choose not to acknowledge the box, the house it is in, the city it is in, or the state it is in.

> *When you say a situation or a person is hopeless, you are slamming the door in the face of God.* — Charles L. Allen

The Invisible Truth is not designed to clinically treat true psychosis. (I am talking about someone with a real split with reality, not any of us here.) It is designed to give the "strivers" in life another tool to add to their journey toward enlightenment. For most of us, looking into the box is a painful thing. The pain radiates at varying levels with each individual.

I know this. When it became apparent to me that I must take the journey through the murky water of my life, I knew there were things in my box that I was very fearful of. This included looking at my past, and the hurt, in order to move forward. The painful events in my life had hindered me from moving to the level I desired. I had allowed my "blocks" to stop me from where I "wanted" to be.

Development of the Invisible Truth did not begin in the last few years with the research being done on the words used here. It started with my acknowledgment that there was the necessity for the journey. For me, that started decades ago. Acknowledging the pain in my life has allowed me to move past the "block" that it created and has given me a much fuller, healthier perspective on life.

It has brought me peace. With peace comes harmony.

None of us are masters. We all have more to learn. My journey has led me to write that which I put before us now. Where is our journey leading us?

Keep going…in the right direction…for the rest of our lives.

By understanding that the process to get to the real truth is lifelong, I am able to move through the process without fear that "I might be missing something" or "I just don't get it. Why hasn't greatness happened yet?" Relax. It will. The important part is the journey.

Now that we have taken responsibility for our life, we are aware of the thoughts and words we use, and our belief system is beginning to alter itself. There may not have been any life altering changes, but we have begun to realize why we believe the things we do. Those beliefs may change altogether. Our belief in our higher power may not have changed, though we may see it with more clarity. Our belief around, say, money, might take a drastic overhaul…in time…as we "stay the course."

As our bucket continues to clear, our work becomes evident. The work of our life may have very little to do with our job, though that is a very good means to an end. We realize the exact role of our current job in the work of our life and it becomes less burdensome.

We are more thankful for the wonderful bounty in our life. This, in turn, leads to giving of our time and effort in ways that will reward us that we don't yet even consider.

While working through the Invisible Truth, we have begun the process of cleansing our environment to rid ourselves of the unnecessary negative energy that has flowed through us…because we allowed it. We have let go of the past and controlled our future by living right now.

Our bucket does not clear itself overnight. It is a lifelong process. It is a journey well worth the effort.

It is a journey to enlightenment.

Go towards the light.

Starting the Journey

This journey begins with memorizing the nine laws and principles of Invisible Truth. In order to synergistically use the laws and principles, we must know what they are.

Live in the Now
Thought (What am I thinking? Be Aware.)
Words (What am I saying? Be Aware.)
Belief (What do I believe? Why? Is what I believe serving me well?)
Work (What is my vision? Is what I am doing right now working toward that vision?)
Being Thankful (Where is my focus? On what I have or what I don't have?)
Forgiveness (Have I forgiven others? Do I forgive myself?)
Giving and Receiving (What do I have to give? Time? Money? Effort? Though I don't give with intent of receiving, I receive with thankfulness in order that I may give more.)
Environment (What and who do I surround myself with?)

The more laws and principles that we have working synergistically together, the stronger the energy force that we put out into the universe.

Energy of the same, or greater, magnitude as that which we put out comes back to us. Abundance is unlimited. And we were given the ability to tap into that divine source of unlimited abundance. Thus, our abundance is unlimited.

Choice

Being aware that I have a choice allows me freedom. I have the freedom to choose what energy I put into any action in my life. I understand that how I react to any given circumstance is fully within my power. I understand that sometimes my choices are limited, but I am free to choose the most desired result I wish to manifest and free to work to create that result.

I am now fully cognizant of my choice to move energy toward freedom to, not freedom from. I understand the vibrational magnitude in the difference between these two concepts.

Consciousness

Becoming aware and conscious allows us to see the water that is flowing into our bucket at all times. It allows us to take the judgment away from our thought patterns and analyze why we think the way we do, and discover more easily all that isn't working in our life…and why it isn't working. This begins the road to change in thought, word and belief.

- What am I thinking and saying?
- Why am I thinking and saying that?
- Is what I am thinking and saying getting me any closer to my desired results?
- If I were standing outside myself and listening to me, how would what I am saying sound? How would it affect me?

- Is what I am hearing doing me any good? Is there good energy in what is being given to me by another? How do I turn what I am hearing into positive energy?
- Am I critical of something that I am seeing and hearing before it, or they, are even done? Have I made a judgment about something based upon my own mud?
- When I am listening to another, am I thinking about my response before they have even finished talking? Am I thinking more about my response than about what they are saying?

Becoming aware and conscious begins with listening to ourselves. Once we begin to listen to ourselves, we will begin to hear others much more clearly. AH-HA moments start coming in such rapid fire succession that we may start to giggle uncontrollably. I have seen it happen. I have done it myself.

My individual consciousness is that which I am aware of. It is the "action" part of my brain. I am now aware that the reactive portion of my brain is my subconscious. It has been put together by all actions, reactions, judgments and emotions I have experienced throughout my life. It has created my "autopilot."

Part of becoming aware is "taking it off autopilot."

As we have discovered, we were on autopilot most of the time. When we take control, autopilot is disengaged. Once we have created the changes in our life, in how we perceive life and all its complexities, the changes become our new autopilot. However, it is critical that, on occasion, a diagnostic be done on our new autopilot system. (How is this working for me?)

However we choose to reprogram the neural pathways of our subconscious is up to us. The laws and principles of Invisible Truth are an effective, time honored, scientifically and philosophically sound method to do so. Use them in congruence and conjunction with each other so that our ultimate goals are attained.

We are now achieving our ultimate goals.

By becoming conscious of our subconscious, and by learning to consciously feed our subconscious in order to manifest our desired reality, we take a huge step toward realizing our God consciousness (universal consciousness or collective unconsciousness...we put our own name to it). We are furthering the possibilities of tapping into that which is unknown. We are breathing the aether.

We are.

The Four Ds

Desire First, we must have the desire to see change in our life. We do...or we would not be at this point in this book.

Determination This is a much bigger concept than desire. Once we have determined that we desire to change our life, we must become absolutely determined that we will change our energy in order to manifest that which we desire. Let me rephrase that, we simply are becoming absolutely determined that we are changing our energy to manifest all that we desire. Simple as that. Our determination has allowed us to clearly see the steps we must take to become prepared for the opportunities that will miraculously appear before us. As we move toward our desire, through preparation, opportunities will become more abundant.

Dedication When we become determined to change our life, we must be absolutely dedicated to doing so. Our dedication and determination become so strong that they are unshaken by the first (or second or third...) "bump in the road" that we hit. We have realized, down to our very core, that change is a lifelong process and with each challenge comes an opportunity. We see the opportunities that arise from any situation. Our focus is no longer on the problem, but on the vast potentials of the solution. We become dedicated to being the cause of the positive effect on the world.

Discipline By far the most challenging of the four Ds. This is where the "rubber meets the road." This is the work portion. This is the "check and balance" of our journey. We have studied the Invisible Truth. We have determined to instill these laws and principles into our life. We have created a plan. We have a vision. We are living in the now, aware of the thoughts and words we are using, and we have evaluated our beliefs and brought them in line with the positive energy of the universe. We have worked through our blocks, are thankful for all that we receive, and have forgiven ourselves and others in our life. We have realized the gifts we give to the world and are grateful for the opportunity to do so. We are in control of our environment and we filled it with the energy we desire.

Discipline is to do all these things every second of every minute of every hour of every day for the rest of our life.

We will slip. We will go to our shadow. Discipline is the awareness that comes from the determination to fight our way back to the light. Whatever it takes, we are doing it. It has taken us this long (however old we are) to create the murk in the bucket. Understand that we will not clear the bucket overnight, but, at every moment, with every thought, with every word, we can enhance the process. Be determined and disciplined in making sure that the hose we have in our bucket at any given time is the clear one.

Discipline is nothing more than being conscious of what is going into our bucket every single second. That's it.

If we see the murk going back into our bucket, we now have the tools to work our way back into the light. Use them. Be disciplined in using them.

Over time, because we are determined thus disciplined, it is no longer an effort. The desire causes the dedication and determination to become so powerful that, soon, the discipline requires no effort. It all starts with a simple desire. We improve each day due to our dedication to that desire.

And therein lies the magic. The work of discipline disappears, with ease, due to the power of the desire. Thus, the goal is attained.

God is perfect. The universe is perfect. With my every breath, I am working my way towards perfection, while remembering that it's not the destination, but the journey.

When I get to the end of this portion of the journey, I am going to look at myself and smile. I have been the best I could be.

Energy

Remember (as if we could forget, we have said it so many times), it is all about energy. The energy we put into the world is that which is attracted back to us. Being aware of the energy we are putting into the world is the first step of attraction. As we become aware of the energy being put into the world we begin to see a shift, without even consciously doing anything more than becoming aware.

One more time, for the record. We are energy. Energy cannot be created or destroyed. The vessel that currently embodies our presence is just that, a vessel.

We understand the principles of cause and effect. We also understand that with effect comes choice. We now understand that we control our reactions to that effect. By controlling our reaction, we now control our "fate." (Our view changes from "it just happened and there was nothing I could do about it" to "it happened and here is what I did about it.")

By redirecting the energy (choice) of that which has come to us, we are now able to direct that energy's flow in a way that will get us closer to where we desire to be, given the circumstance. Once we have taken control of the redirection of energy, we now control its direction, thereby becoming the cause, not the effect. We control our own destiny.

Feeding Our Soul (Feeding the Senses of Our Soul First)

Because we are energy, we are part of the universe. Because we are conscious energy, we are a soul. Handle it.

Being a part of the universe means that we are greater than the vessel currently carrying us...get over it.

It is, therefore, our responsibility to feed our soul at an even higher rate than we feed the vessel that currently carries it. Don't get me wrong, it is imperative that we take the best care possible of our bodies. What I am saying is that it is even more imperative that we take good care of our soul.

Do not do what others have done (people I have known in my life). Do not get to the end of life as we currently know it and ask..."what if I was wrong?"

If feeding our soul means being at church every Sunday, then that is what is right for us. If it means helping at the food bank twice a month, good for us. If it means hang gliding over the ocean bluff...more power to us.

If it means doing cocaine and drinking whisky...it is time for a rethink.

God is in me. I don't have to go far; I just have to let Him out. (Sure beats running after the right religion, hoping the church or shrine or temple or synagogue I was currently attending was the only one that would get me to the pearly gates.)

Wherever we find peace...wherever we find community...wherever we find love...that is our sanctuary. Revel in it. Thrive in it. Give thanks in it. Let Him out...and smile.

I choose not to live my life amongst the seven deadly sins and I do not focus on them. Wrath, greed, pride, lust, gluttony, sloth and envy go directly against God's will. Therefore, they go directly against my soul. The energy is so negative in these words that they lead to desperation, anguish, depression and despair. Just writing these words is a dark energy. However, I am not naive nor do I pretend these things do not exist. They do. But, they have no valid part of my existence.

I choose to put my energy around the wonder of love, discipline, charity, generosity, diligence, forgiveness, patience, admiration, kindness and humility. Look at the light in these words. Living with the energy of these concepts in my life is leading me to live within the Invisible Truth...Thy will be done, on earth as it is in heaven.

Create here, on this plane of existence, that which we wish to carry into the next life.

Don't be fooled. Read the teachings of the ancients accurately...understand the laws of the universe. We are energy. The energy we create right here, right now, is the energy that carries though with us to the next plane. If we choose to create nothing but negative energy, do we actually believe that we will get a reprieve from that energy in the next life? Guess again. Our energy carries through to that existence as well...and the learning will start all over.

It's Karma, baby....

What is it that we must do that is so important as to go against the energy of the universe and the laws of God? A rethink may be in order.

Feeding our soul first means doing whatever it is that we enjoy doing...whatever it is that brings us (real) peace. Inevitably, whatever that thing is, we are bringing joy and peace to others as well. There are words wrapped around that "thing" that sound something like teaching, giving, playing, learning and laughing. The resulting words sound like gladness, contentedness, peacefulness...satisfaction.

Do the right thing. Do the right thing. Do the right thing.

Soothing the Soul. Visualization. Meditation.

We all get going so fast in our lives, with so many responsibilities, that taking time for ourselves is not really high on the priority list. I understand that. In fact, I find it difficult to slow down at any point in the day until I hit sheer exhaustion. I am not going to say that I have mastered the reflective posture that many have. I am working on it.

I know how to meditate and what works for me when I actually do it. Do I do it a lot? No. However, I have developed a system that works for me.

When I am doing an autopilot function...taking a shower, washing the dishes, eating my lunch...I consciously drift toward a mental picture of where I desire to be. I see it in my mind. I smell it, taste it and feel it in my mind. I see myself functioning within the atmosphere I have created in my mind. I have visualized it.

For me, what that looks like is a place of harmony.

The peace that I feel usually dictates the vision of the places I enjoy. The visions involve my home, the mountains, the places I feel comfortable. I am surrounded by a feeling of wellbeing and security. I am surrounded by the material objects that bring me joy. My visions do not involve lots of stuff, but there are things (material objects) that bring me satisfaction.

What I get most from my visions is the feeling of comfort with those I surround myself with in my vision. I am financially free with multiple streams of income. I have also found the joy of the work that I do. I am clear on what my life's work is and revel in doing it. It allows me to give to the world in a way that I find quite gratifying, which is a reward in itself. My visualization is one of peace. Keeping that vision allows me to move towards it in a subconscious way.

When I do take the time to meditate, I find a calm place in my environment where I will not be disturbed. The first thing I do is turn off my cell phone. (The world will get by without me for 10 minutes.) I sit in a place where the view is one I appreciate and enjoy. I start by clearing my head. That is achieved by concentrating on my breathing. When I have my breathing under control, I simply turn on the projector.

In my mind there come pictures, seemingly randomly. However, unlike a movie, this is interactive. I control the content of the pictures as they come to me. I take the energy of the image and change it to that which I desire. When I am done, I say so to myself, and I come back to my center through my breathing. This is not a long, drawn out process. A long and complex image and manipulation may take thirty seconds. Most of the time, it is a matter of a few seconds. Much of the time I am concentrating on my breathing. Sometimes my eyes are closed and sometimes they are open. Usually when I have a view of Mt. Rainier, my eyes never leave the mountain. (I know that God is in me, but I am pretty convinced that He is living on that mountain too.)

In a space of 10 minutes, I stand up with a new perspective, feeling calmer.

I drive around the city of Seattle a lot in my work. As far as I am concerned, this is one of the most beautiful places on the planet…as long as a person is not afraid of getting wet. The point is that there are some very scenic vistas all over this city, and when I am feeling agitated, or in my shadow, sometimes I simply pull over (to a safe parking area), stare at the scene in front of me and meditate for two minutes.

I always feel better and have a different perspective when I am done. It does not take hours and hours and huge amounts of training to do this. In fact, I don't even call it meditating (the term always sounded a little too distant to me). I call it "clearing the mechanism." I got that from the movie, *For the Love of the Game*, with Kevin Costner playing the aging pitcher, Billy Chapel. The term stuck. It is the term his character uses to find focus…to move away from being inside his own head. To dispassionately observe the events of his life...without judgment or emotion. I like it. I use it. It is now an integral part of my inner game.

Anyway, it is a good thing to "clear the mechanism" on occasion. It allows us the opportunity to see things as they are...as they truly are...without all the emotion and judgment wrapped around the issue.

Find a way to "clear the mechanism." As we are clearing the mechanism, use the laws and principles to harmoniously find the path we choose to walk. Remember to integrate all of the laws and principles into our vision. Create our vision.

We are finding all that we desire. We have gotten out of our own way. We have found freedom, joy...and peace. Harmony. We have found the Invisible Truth.

Action Steps for the Week

- Live in the real truth, the Invisible Truth.

Romans 1:20 For since the creation of the world God's invisible qualities—his eternal power and divine nature—have been clearly seen, being understood from what has been made, so that men are without excuse. (NIV)

The Last Words

You may call me a dreamer
But I'm not the only one
I hope someday you'll join us
And the world will live as one.
— John Lennon 1971

The mass of men lead lives of quiet desperation and go to the grave with the song still in them. — Henry David Thoreau

However we define it, we came from God. From the moment of our birth we spend the rest of our lives either running back to or running away from Him. All we are doing is running towards or running away from ourselves.

Now that we understand the Invisible Truth, it is in our charge. Let God out. Live our song. Touch the world and the universe. Bring peace.

When it is time for me to face myself and to face my God, I will be smiling. I will be ready for my next adventure. I will have sung my song.

Join the choir.

Our Stance

The powerful words within this text are not mine. The message is one that has already been written, already been spoken, already been taught. The lessons put into this book are the compilation of the teachings of the ancients, as well as the thoughts of the wise ones of our times.

I did not write these words, these laws of the universe. In fact, I didn't even put these thoughts together. The thoughts and beliefs put into the new dynamics presented here are the result of many meritorious minds. Preachers, pastors, ministers, scholars, teachers, philosophers, scientists, physicists, anthropologists and everyone in between, practicing or not practicing the tenets of Christianity, Judaism, Taoism, Buddhism, Hinduism, Islam, agnosticism and atheism.

The words we have read are affecting me in the same way they have affected all of us. I am saying this to assure all of us here that this is not being written by a "master." However, the more I read and researched, the more I began to realize just how powerful these lessons are. These nine Laws and Principles are changing my life.

The change continues. Every day I see how these lessons make me a better person.

Using the religious teachings I was raised with, I put forward these facts. The Bible tells us that the Kingdom of God is within us. (Luke 17:20-21) The Bible also tells us that to enter the Kingdom of God we are to be born again. (John 3:3) Those who follow the logic of the Bible will see it in a reinvigorated form. It is a form that empowers us to see and understand our potential as a human race.

If God is all knowing, all powerful and ever present, and the Kingdom of God is within us, all we have to do is accept it and we tap into the potential far beyond our limited understanding. To deny this is to deny God.

Do we deny God?

I am awakened and reborn each day. Every day I am born again with renewed life. With conscious choice I move forward with directed, organized energy to create positive change in my life and in the universe. I move energy in a directed, organized method that I consciously control. With practice, I create positive results in my life and in the universe with laser precision. .

It is invigorating.

Using the basic teachings of science from my middle school years, I know that everything I can think of, including the thought I just had, is made up of energy. Of all the elements in the universe, there is one thing that is an absolute, the concept of energy. I was taught that energy cannot be destroyed, nor can it be created. It can, however, be changed and directed.

I was taught that the molecules that make up energy, or anything for that matter, had an attraction factor and a repulsion factor. Those molecules that had the same or similar energy charges tended to attract each other. Those molecules with dissimilar energy charges tend to repel each other.

In very simplistic language, when I put these two things together that I learned growing up, I came to the following conclusions. When I accept that God is energy, and therefore the Universe (which God made) is energy, and that the Kingdom of God, and therefore the potential for the understanding of the power of God, is within me, then I have the power within myself to change the universe around me.

God's energy is within me. Therefore, I can use directed, organized energy to cause real changes in my life.

The philosopher Rene Descartes said, "I think, therefore I am." Taking this one step further, it is clearer that "I am what I think I am."

It is accepted that thought is energy, and that energy cannot be destroyed, only altered. Then, is it possible that the current vessel which contains our thoughts is only a temporary embodiment of a universal consciousness? If so, is it possible that the energy that flows through us in the form of random, compulsive, disorganized energy, which creates havoc in our lives, can be redirected in a controlled, positive way? The answer is yes.

We can be consciously changed by moving energy to attract that which we desire to attract in this life. Think about it. Or, should I say, create energy around that? We have all heard about people's auras. Could it be that the aura we create emanates from us as a visualization of our power and energy?

The ties between science and faith have been dismissed for centuries by thoughtful men. This book is not an "end all" for the conclusive study finally settling the matter. There will always be smart people who feel the need to argue these points. However, those who limit themselves to only the potentials of what they have been taught do not have the answer. They don't have the answer because there isn't one. The answer exists when all that can ever be known about faith and science is known. By definition, that is never going to happen, at least within the vessel that carries us in this lifetime.

If it did happen, do we know what we would call ourselves? God.

Dan Brown wrote a book called *The Lost Symbol* that spoke of the emerging study of Noetic Science. It is a good novel. That is just what it is though, a novel. However, in the book he poses some interesting questions regarding the way in which we have faced our teachings. Specifically, he talks of the parables used in the Bible, and the interpretations of the "teachers" of those parables. In all major philosophies and religions of the world there are some very basic premises and rules about how we treat God (or whatever our faith calls our Supreme Being), ourselves (this bundle of conscious energy), and others around us.

In the book, Mr. Brown also makes several salient points which I will focus on here. Using the Bible as an example, Jesus told his followers on several occasions that the teachings of the Bible were told in parables. A parable is a story designed to teach a truth, principle or moral lesson. It gives meaning to truth in an indirect way through comparison. It is, therefore, left to us to figure out what the lesson is.

Matthew 13:34-35 Jesus spoke all these things to the crowd in parables; he did not say anything to them without using a parable. So was fulfilled what was spoken through the prophet: "I will open my mouth in parables, I will utter things hidden since the creation of the world."(NIV)

What if the parables were written in code to protect us from the actual meaning of the holy writings?

Could it be that those who have taught us the meanings behind the parables, and those who taught them, etc., twisted the meaning to their truth? What would happen if the real code of the Bible or Torah or Koran or Vedic teachings or Tao or any of the other teachings of this earth were all done through a secret message system like the parables, and therefore encoded for us to figure out?

What if it was decided by others (the churches) that the truth shall be hidden? What if the teachings have been given to us in a way that does not clearly convey the actual lessons of the holy writings?

What if the blasphemy, as is declared by those of closed minds, is not blasphemy at all?

What if God IS in us…and it is up to us to let Him out to do His work? His work is our work.

His work is the Law of the Universe. His is the Law of Science. His scriptures are the works given to us as an avenue by which we may find the laws of the universe.

The arguments I have put forth to my peers as I have struggled through my own faith were these: God (the Holy Spirit) is in me, He says so. Therefore, if God is in me, does that mean that I am, in a word, God? It is my stance that if I were to tap into all of the resources God allowed me, could I, conceivably, become God-like?

This argument was thrown out by many of my contemporaries, peers, teachers and mentors as blasphemous. Why? What are they afraid of? Is it fear that by getting closer to God I might take full control of my own life? My own choices, my actions, my destiny. My afterlife. Take control instead of following orders from the pulpit?

It has been taught that I am here to do God's work. Fine, I get that. It is also taught that I have freewill. I get that too. What if my freewill does not dictate that I move away from God (as some of my debaters state), but that freewill was given to me to use as a tool to find the true meaning encoded in the holy writings?

Freewill is "Freedom to, not freedom from." It is freedom to choose God's way, for myself, not freedom from God's ways. It is freedom to be good for good's sake, not freedom from "punishment for eternity" as a driving force for us to use as an excuse to make ourselves behave. The intent is to be free.

The guilt foisted on us by certain religions, the threat of damnation, has caused many to mistakenly choose freewill as their religion which, in turn, has led to the choice of pleasures of the flesh and the pursuit of the seven deadly sins. The lessons have been so misconstrued by those who have pompously taught them that the world has turned its back on organized, old school religions.

Through history there have been some religions in this world that have misinterpreted the meanings of their "holy book" in such a wicked way that people were ready to murder others, just for the sake of killing, because of what they were taught was the actual and real meaning of "their" scriptures. In addition, they have been taught that they get a bonus for killing others in the name of "their" God. Their illogical rationalization is that they would be guaranteed a place in "their heaven."

Every church, that bears repeating, every established church of every organized religion has committed atrocities.

I tell you what…if I had been taught throughout my life that the God I believed in was condoning me slaughtering innocents, I would only hope that I would take a different view of what was being taught, or the way it was being taught. I could only hope that I would lead the very vocal protest. It is time to break this cycle.

The sins of the church, temple, synagogue, shrine, mosque, wherever we speak to our creator of our universe, are no less severe than the sins of those living outside their doors. We, as well as the church, must know the difference between right and wrong.

At the same time, churches and religions of all types are filled with enlightened individuals. Some are actually breaking free of the dogma and exploring the vast possibilities of their faith. This isn't about the church. This is about us. When we discover that God is actually in us, it gives us the freedom to use the church as an avenue to explore all of the potentials, realizing that theirs is one of limitless possibilities. Freedom to, not freedom from. Doing the right thing.

Who (which church or religion) is right? Who cares? God is in YOU. Turn around and face your God, for yourself.

I can't buy my way to God. I can't just pray my way to God. Prayer without works is empty. I can, however, let Him out to do His work.

Getting to God means living correctly right now: being pure in thought and word; believing what is good and right; working hard to attain our vision of righteousness; being thankful for all we have; forgiving others as we would ask to be forgiven; giving to the world with a thankful heart and controlling the environment in which we live, thus creating "Heaven on Earth," by living in our own inner peace. This is the way to God.

If we see what the holy writings are actually saying…if we see how science backs up the actual meaning of the scriptures…a whole new meaning to what has been taught will come to us.

Some have taken the meaning of freewill to be an allowance to make up their own minds about the deciphering of the holy teachings. Inevitably, these are the people drawn closer to God, not further apart. And, they aren't killing anyone for the sake of "their God." They aren't preaching in the morning and sinning the rest of the day. They aren't driving confused parishioners away from the church with hypocrisy and fear of damnation.

Some choose to exercise their freewill to do good because they know it feels right. They are letting God out, not keeping God out. They understand the science of their faith. And they walk amongst us.

It is inconceivable to me that there are those out there who actually believe that God is sitting on His righteous, far away cloud deciding who is right and who is wrong.

The scriptures read that God is in us. In the moment we meet our maker, guess who we will be facing first?

Look in the mirror.

It is the contention of Invisible Truth that we have been looking for the difference between science and faith, rather than the similarities, and that logic that brings these together.

I choose freewill to find God within me and get Him working in my life. God made us in His form and likeness.

He never intended for us to be sheep.

No matter how we say it, define it or speculate about it, the basis, the very axis of life, all comes down to one general principle. Love. Love, arguably, is the greatest energy that exists in all of the universe.

Mark 12:30-31 Love the Lord your God with all your heart and with all your soul and with all your mind and with all your strength. The second is this: 'Love your neighbor as yourself.' There is no commandment greater than these. (NIV)

It can be argued that the only reason mankind has survived the follies of being human is because of love. The instinctual survival of this species, and all other species we know of, is due to the inherent love we have for those we bring into the world. How else are we going to explain it?

I have written the things I have learned in a way that, to me, makes sense. These are not my thoughts alone, not by a long shot. As the old saying goes, "there is nothing new under the sun." This is one person's interpretation of the conclusions of many people who have, in their own way, found answers to questions that have been with man since the beginning of time.

I have compiled a great deal of research which brought me to the conclusion that the actual differences between science and religion are in the semantics.

Semantics.

Having led a life of questioning, I have concluded that science and faith are one in the same. The attempts to date to bring these facts to light have been faulted, ignored or left incomplete. In no way do I state that I have the answers. My conclusions have, however, led me to a more direct question about the mysteries of the universe.

Is it blasphemy?

Finding the right answers can be elusive. There are, however, right questions. The answers we come to are ours. The seekers in this life have striven to find the answers and there are many "teachers" who wish to provide them. The questions that have arisen, at least for me, have brought frustration, wonder and more questions. As I have continued to ask questions, the conclusions I have drawn have narrowed my questions to those that I can accept.

I have personally sought the answers to life, death, my soul, Heaven, hell, science, and the mysteries of the universe since I was old enough to understand the teachings being offered, and look into the night sky and gaze beyond the stars. It seemed the more I studied, the more questions I had. The work contained here didn't necessarily give me the answers.

What it did do, however, was to begin to clarify the questions.

This begins with becoming aware of what we don't know. By forming the questions, we move forward with clarity. We have begun the process of actualization and manifestation.

An exponential reaction: multiplication, not addition.

I am a loving mother of two amazing, and amusing, children. I am a successful businesswoman and a musician. I truly enjoy the art of the written word, both absorbing and creating. These are just a few of the things I am. I do have fun with my life.

Having been introduced to Invisible Truth's laws and principles, I am now able to state these things with true confidence and with authority. I am at peace. This wasn't always the way. It is now.

Yes, I slip. I slip into the darkness of my shadow on occasion. I slip into that dark place…you know the one. The difference is now I see it for what it is. I recognize it. By seeing it, I am able to begin the steps I require to bring myself back to the light instead of staying in the dark. Now, I reach out instead of draw in. I am a warrior.

The real accomplishment in life is the art of being a warrior, which is the only way to balance the terror of being a man with the wonder of being a man. — Carlos Castaneda

When it comes time for me to meet my maker, I will not be confused. Of course, it is my faith that when that time comes the answers will be evident anyway. That doesn't keep me from working toward finding the right questions.

Again, I am stating for the record, these are not my words.

They are your words. Your questions. Your life.

…How's it going for you now…your life, that is?

Part Three

Putting It All Together

Cosmic Consciousness

Science without religion is lame, religion without science is blind.
— Albert Einstein, "Science, Philosophy and Religion: a
Symposium," 1941

We touched upon the concept of aether in the first pages, now
we'll continue to explore this span of "the void."

Aether

Though they were not the first, ancient Greek philosophers stated
that the classic elements of the states of matter were Earth, Water,
Fire and Air. In addition to that, there is a fifth element...Aether.
The concept of aether (ey-ther; "ey" is pronounced as a long A, as
in shape) is relatively hard to define. Aristotle and Plato wrote of
the concept, however, it is not a principle unique to any of the
great thinkers or philosophies throughout history.

Aether, in some definitions, is thought of as the "void" through
which all other elements were created or travel. The concept is
widely taught, or thought of, in Hinduism, Jainism, Buddhism and
other great religions of the world.

A current, Western religious philosophy called Theosophy, with
ambassadors as prominent as Plato, has adopted the basic tenets of
the fifth element, as have numerous other Eastern and Western
religious ideologies.

The modern ideologies say the aether touches us; some call it the
aura which touches or surrounds or emanates from within the

human body. Some "see" the aura as the energy emanating from within.

Greek mythological traditions hold that aether is the pure, fresh air that the Gods breathe. It is thought that mortals can breathe the same air, and thereby are able to tap into the same understanding of the universe as the Gods, if they only can see things for what they are. This is called, by some, God consciousness.

Theosophy uses a term called Akashic (ah-kah-sheek) records, whose basis is in the Hindu philosophy, that refers to the recording of all the energy of thought, word and action throughout time. Some philosophies call this the cosmic or collective consciousness. Aether is thought of as the void through which this energy travels... through which all energy travels. And has always traveled. And always will.

In other words...energy cannot be created nor destroyed. It can be changed. The cosmic consciousness records all the changes of energy throughout the universe for all of eternity. Some people call this God. Some call it universal consciousness. Some call it the collective consciousness.

We are energy. The universe is energy. We are a part of the collective consciousness. The knowledge we gain from the collective consciousness is brought to us through the medium we call aether. The medium of aether is defined as a fine gas made up of the smallest particles of matter. These particles carry information from point A to point B faster than the speed of light. Even the invisible space between us is made up of energy; it too is part of the medium.

Some men of science define aether as the transmission medium. Einstein was one of these great minds. He developed this, as a crucial factor, within one of his two versions of his theory of relativity.

Energy travels via a medium. Energy, such as sound, travels from one bundle of conscious energy (you) to another (me) across the medium (void or air) with audible vibrations (energy).

Different ideologies, doctrines and philosophies say these words in different ways. The bottom line is this. Western religions expound upon the fact that the knowledge brought to "an individual faith" is gained through a medium called the Holy Spirit (or Holy Ghost). Knowledge gained through the collective energy of the universe is brought to us through the transmission medium of aether.

Same concept, different words.

Romans 15:13 May the God of hope fill you with all joy and peace as you trust in him, so that you may overflow with hope by the power of the Holy Spirit. (NIV)

Ponder that. Every thought we have, every single thing we do, is recorded throughout posterity. I give thanks that this life isn't the end, but merely a part of the whole, simply an alteration of the energy. Independent religions have different ideas about what happens in the "afterlife." Science shows that we are all bundles of conscious energy; energy changes form. It is not created nor destroyed. There is a definite correlation here.

All of life is related to the movement of energy.

Aether. Cosmic Consciousness. We know that this concept exists and is real in sciences and in religions.

Each of us has a different awareness of what death brings. Those who state that they know what happens after our hearts stop beating are stating their own thesis, opinion or theory.

The wonder of the universe and the things I now understand lead me to the conclusion that the vessel that currently embodies my soul is a temporary manifestation of my actual being.

I am energy. Energy cannot be created nor destroyed. It does, however, change forms. Therefore, my being, if made up of energy, does not cease its existence upon death of my physical body; it only changes forms.

Theories of Aether

Whatever our Supreme Source is, there is a medium through which that source communicates with us. If we are Christians, that source is the Holy Spirit. For a Buddhist, that source is the chakras. The force of the Tao is qi (or ki or chi). If we are Hindu, it is the akash. In psychology, Carl Jung actually touched closely to this with his "collective unconsciousness." In Japanese philosophies, it is Kū (or sora), which, again, is translated as "void."

Studied further, it includes the more common definitions of "sky" and "Heaven"; it also indicates power, creativity and pure energy. In martial arts, it is explained as the quintessential creative energy; when one is attuned to the void then one can sense that which exists in their surroundings and act accordingly, without stopping to think, without requiring the physical senses, just responding appropriately.

If we are scientists, that source is aether (and ether).

Albert Einstein, one of the leaders and founders of the quantum theory and quantum mechanics, argued that there was a certain unknown factor that could not be measured and was beyond the understanding of science, and he set out to produce a series of objections to his theory of relativity. He put a name to that which could not be explained, aether (ether). Essentially, he wrote two versions of the theory of relativity, both with and without aether, a highly contested factor in the scientific universe.

Modern science has seen a resurgence of this concept of aether. The intrigue is that, for time immemorial, science has continued to work on this concept. The current ventures are to develop a mathematically correct Unified Force Theory, explanations of dark matter, and how physical matter interacts with consciousness.

In the last decades, physics held no exact concept of aether. There was work on aether as quintessence which is defined as: 1. the pure and concentrated essence of a substance. 2. the most perfect embodiment of something. 3. (in ancient and medieval philosophy) the fifth essence or element, ether, supposed to be the constituent matter of the heavenly bodies, the others being air, fire, earth and water.[1]

Within the current study of aether, modern physics continues to work on the concepts of dark matter, free space, spin foam, Planck particles, quantum wave state, zero-point energy, quantum foam, and vacuum energy.[2] (Boy, there is a tongue twister of words I don't have any desire to decipher....)

Earlier modern physicists and alchemists considered aether to be a transmission medium. A commonality was the theory that aether existed everywhere in space and in all materials.

The physics definition of aether is a hypothetical substance supposed to occupy all space, postulated to account for the propagation of electromagnetic radiation through space.

And propagation is defined as to create (an effect) at a distance, as by electromagnetic waves, compression waves, etc., traveling through space or a physical medium. Given enough time, from a hypothesis a scientist will collect facts sufficient enough to prove or disprove a premise.

Transmission medium...electromagnetic propagation...through space or a physical medium. Okay, I don't precisely know what all of those words mean, but this is sure sounding like aether to me.

Science and religion are describing the exact same concept.

Some say that the abandonment of ether by science led to its eventual abandonment of aether by spiritualists and theosophists. I say that, despite the lack of conclusions in concrete, I hear a lot of brilliant minds around the world still chewing on the same concept. Aether.

All of these words, indeed all of these discussions, are related to the movement of energy. Not what it moves, but how it moves. More specifically, aether is the unknown through which energy moves in forms that are not material, definable or physical.

In other words, aether is the idea of an idea.

It is the cosmic venue through which we pass the energy of an idea into space…and thereby into another bundle of conscious energy, and how that bundle of conscious energy processes it and passes it on into the next directional energy change. It is not the energy change itself, but the venue through which energy is passed that will, in turn, redirect energy in a physical way.

Yes. "The next directional energy change…."

An Example: Instinct

Have you ever been in a situation where your instinct tugged on you to do, or not do, something and there was no logical or deductive reasoning behind your instinct? Usually this concept is wrapped around your "not doing something" when there is no evidence whatsoever that would cause you to conclude that doing that the action would cause harm.

A woman I know, Monica, told me a story about her instinct once. She was walking though a park early in the morning with her friend. This was Monica's normal morning workout. They approached a bend in the path. Monica began to slow as she experienced an overwhelmingly foreboding feeling. For no known reason, she felt that there was something around the corner that was a threat to her. Her friend had no clue as to why, and for a few paces kept moving at the accelerated pace…happily talking away. Monica grabbed her friend and turned them both around, to head back in the direction they had come from. They had both walked this path in the past so they knew nothing unique existed around that corner. They had travelled only a few hundred yards back away from it when they came across a park ranger. He told them that there had been an incidence of violence just hours before, right around the bend from where they had stopped, and that the perpetrator had not yet been apprehended.

How did she know to stop?

We all have "gut instinct." Using Monica's experience as an example, she felt the negative energy that emanated from the place that had recently been the scene of a violent act. Because she was tapped into her God consciousness, collective consciousness, whatever we wish to call it, she potentially saved her friend and herself from harm. The collective consciousness had recorded an incident in a specific location which vibrated negative energy. Aether was the medium through which she received her "premonition." She acted on those instincts in the proper manner. She listened to her "gut."

How many times have we all said…I wish I had listened to my gut? How many times have we gone against our instinct and it turned out our instinct was right? Every time?

Our God consciousness is diluted through our own process of thought and rationalized reasoning. The right thing is the right thing is the right thing…and this goes well beyond what our parents taught us and what we learned in kindergarten. Unless we are in denial, or over-think any situation, or rationalize our evil intent, our God consciousness always knows the proper action in any given situation; it is given to us through the aether.

A scientist would call this inductive reasoning. Inductive reasoning is that which is logic dictated, understanding that there are unknown elements within the decision making process. These decisions are inclusive of the unknown, based on past experience and observation. To make this clearer, the inverse is deductive reasoning, in which conclusions are drawn from facts that are present, all variables are known.

An example. In my town, all the fire hydrants *that I have observed* are painted green. Deductive reasoning is that the fire hydrants I have observed in this town are green therefore the oddly formed structure in front of me that looks like a fire hydrant, even though it only has two nozzle valve openings instead of three, is the right height and width, is connected to the city water system, and is painted green, therefore, must be a fire hydrant.

Inductive reasoning states all of the fire hydrants I have observed in this town are green, therefore all fire hydrants in this town are painted green. The first conclusion I have drawn from observation, the second from inference.

The space between an experience with known factors, and that which could not possibly be known through any experience, or observation, when a decision is made that is not based on known factors, is due to us acting upon our instinct; it is our tapping into our God consciousness.

To get really fancy with words that, until I began writing this, and using the fire hydrants as an example, I did not utilize in daily conversation…"a posteriori" reasoning concludes that the fire hydrants I have observed in this town are green, therefore I can conclude that all fire hydrants are green. (I have seen them and judged that all that I have seen were painted the same color.) From the facts, we can deduce a theory by which we can define an order for the reality around us. "A priori" reasoning concludes that I believe that all the fire hydrants in this town are, by law, supposed to be painted the same color green, therefore, even though I have not seen all the fire hydrants, I know that I will recognize them all because they are all green. From the theory, we can infer, or predict, the facts we will most probably see.

A posteriori reasoning says that from my observations I can develop a theory while a priori reasoning says I have a theory, a belief, from which I can predict my observations.

Again, bear with me…there is a point to all this.

It is generally concluded (depending on whose study we are reading) that mankind uses no more than 20 percent of our brain at any given time. That is the most generous estimate; they range between two percent and 20 percent. Honestly, two percent is the most commonly accepted maximum that we access. (Okay, if we think we are so smart, why do we keep losing our keys?)

Think of it this way. Assuming that we are not on a treadmill right now, how much of our bodily muscle capacity are we using while reading this? Though we have muscle throughout our body, rarely, if ever, do we use the full capacity of our muscles all at once. Even when exercising vigorously, certain and specific muscles are not all being used; some are conserving energy. The only time humans seem to use all their muscles at once is in the "fight or flight" scenarios when our very existence is in jeopardy.

These are the times when we hear that someone will manifest "superhuman" strength to get out of a situation they are in…or die.

It is the same with the brain. However, scientists have concluded that even when we are exercising our brains to full capacity, we are nowhere near using 100 percent of our actual capacity. In fact, it is always and inevitably thought of as being a disproportionately small portion of our brain that we use, even when we are thinking at our most proficient level.

We have all seen examples of people who have been born with brains that operate differently in the most basic of functions from that of the "normal" people. We have also seen evidence of people whose brains learned to "reroute" signals to accomplish the desired objective. Think of the savants (the movie *Rainman*…if you haven't seen it, rent it) you have been astounded by. Think of the people who have had brain injuries who have learned to walk or talk all over again.

They rerouted the neural pathways of their brains to relocate the commands of their bodily functions. This, by itself, shows that our brain's capacity is still a mystery. As theorized, if it is 90 to 98 percent unused then I should be able to make the quantum leap to being able to choose to employ more of my brain space for increased physical prowess, speed or hand to eye coordination. Right?

So, there is a great deal of gray matter between our ears not being utilized at any given time. At a certain point in our physical development, the actual number of brain cells we have stops multiplying. Therefore, the development of our brain and its capacity to think and assimilate is not merely a function of growth, but of use. It is a muscle whose capacity is far greater than any of the other muscles of our body and is only defined by our own, self-imposed thought patterns (neural pathways) of limitations.

Were Einstein, Plato, Aristotle, Lincoln, Freud or any of the other colossal thinkers in history any different than we are? Well…maybe. Perhaps they were genetically predisposed to being able to access one tenth of a percent more of their unutilized brain matter than we are. Let me put it to us this way. It isn't that we don't or can't comprehend that which they conceived; given enough study time, it is just the fact that we didn't think of it first.

1 Corinthians 2:13-14 This is what we speak, not in words taught us by human wisdom but in words taught by the Spirit, expressing spiritual truths in spiritual words. The man without the Spirit does not accept the things that come from the Spirit of God, for they are foolishness to him, and he cannot understand them, because they are spiritually discerned. (NIV)

What if…what if…what if that excess brain matter is, actually, working for us in a way that science does not understand? What if that part of our brain is actually underutilized due to our own self-imposed limitations? What if that is the part of our brain that is the potential connection to the collective consciousness? What if that part of our brain is the part that has stored, or has the capacity to tap into, all the knowledge, wisdom and lessons throughout time?

What if that is where God lives?

Our Physical Senses

The senses of the physical world are sight, touch, smell, hearing and taste. Through these we build the empirical evidence of our world. If it looks like a fire, feels hot, smells smoky, sounds and consumes like a fire, then it is a fire. Deductive thought. Therefore, all fires are hot thus they should not be touched. A posteriori reasoning.

Inference allows us to assume that because we know the concept that "all fires are hot," then each fire we experience is, indeed, hot, thus we know not to touch the next fire we see, years later, because it too will be hot. Through inductive thought, we know that all fire is hot. A priori reasoning.

These conclusions we can understand. They are scientifically based and backed with empirical evidence. Then, how do we explain the phenomena that cannot be explained through empirical evidence? How did Monica know not to go around the bend in that park?

See if we can explain these: gut instinct, a gut reaction, a mother's instinct, "the hairs on the back of our neck stood up," "I just knew" the moment I saw him, women's intuition, "I visualized the finished product," it was just déjà vu, or "I never gave up my attempts because I believed I was right." For that matter, how do we explain faith?

For the purpose of this instinct definition here, I am assuming we're speaking of true instinctive reactions. Science can irrevocably explain away many quasi-instinct examples. If we "saw his shadow out of the corner of our eye," "read somewhere that there are numerous poisonous mushrooms," or "heard that rationale in a movie or in a childhood tale," then there is a purely logical reason why we would suddenly ascertain the seemingly miraculous conclusion. That exemplifies pure, simple logic. We are not talking about that here.

Logic, at its most basic premise, is about deductive and inductive reasoning. Through experience and experimentation in our own lives, we have concluded that "if this happens, then that will happen." However, the conclusions drawn in our minds are, by their very nature, limiting. Because of experience, clouded by judgment wrapped in emotion, we have deduced that "if this happens, then that will happen," when, in fact, the outcome of the "this leading to that" may not be the natural outcome at all. We cannot stop the "this" from happening, and in some cases, cannot keep the "that" from then happening. What we can do, however, is to control the next "that" by creating a new "this," based on the previous "that." I'll explain.

Cause and effect are a never ending chain of events that, in our lives, create what is commonly thought of as "fate." However, the word "fate" connotes that we really don't have any control over the events that describe our circumstance. This is not true. We may not have control of the original cause…or effect, for that matter. We do have control over the next cycle within the chain of events stemming from the original cause.

In terms of being human, not necessarily in the world of mathematics, if cause A happens leading to effect B, then cause B will lead to effect C. We cannot control effect B. We can, however, control the variables leading from effect B to how we create cause B, which will then dictate effect C, and so on. The space between effect B and cause B is the space of freewill.

It is the "freedom to, not freedom from" factor.

Let's put this another way. If A then B, if B then C. Instead of C, we choose D. Instead of becoming the effect (C) of the first effect (B), we choose to proactively become the cause (D) of the next effect (E), instead of being a mere effect, which is what we're accustomed to being or what we call fate or the inevitable. Therein lies the premise of Invisible Truth.

Are our heads reeling yet? Don't worry. It gets a lot more lucid as we move on.

Okay, if you yell at me (A) I sulk (B), then you get mad and give me the silent treatment (C). Instead, let's choose to alter the energy flow. When you yell at me (A), I lift my head back up the moment it starts to droop while I consider your point of view (my new B which we'll call D) and agree that we are both right (we'll also call this D) so that you instantly calm down and continue rationally discussing the issue with me like mature adults (E) which I enjoy immensely, and I learn more about you in the resultant conversation.

How Invisible Truth Fits in

It is the contention of Invisible Truth that by opening our minds to all of the possibilities within the realm of potential consequence, we are tapping into the God consciousness.

It is further contended that, not only can we open our minds to all possibilities, we can also tap into the positive collective energy of the universe and thereby create the results we deeply desire.

The universe is made up of energy, a given. We, as humans, are bundles of conscious energy, a given. Energy cannot be created nor destroyed, but can be redirected, a given.

The key word here is redirected…control.

God created the law of free will, and God created the law of cause and effect. And he himself will not violate the law. We need to be thinking less in terms of what God did and more in terms of whether or not we are following those laws.
— Marianne Williamson

We control energy, an empirical fact. We choose to control energy, via freewill.

Could it be that the philosophies and religions of man are nothing more than the interpretations of the teachings of the Supreme Being on how to control the energy of the universe? That those teachings are nothing more than the method through which we tap into God consciousness and the energy of the universe…all the wisdom of the ages?

Some Logic and Some What Ifs

Our brains underutilize their capacity, a given. Because we are made up of energy, and the universe is made up of energy, we are part of the universe's energy, a given.

The possibility that Invisible Truth puts forward is this: if the universe is composed of energy which includes everything that has ever happened and that will ever happen, including all of faith and all of science, and that we are part of that collective…what if we were to utilize the remaining 98 percent of our brain's capacity and tap into the collective consciousness?

What if we were to do so simply by deciding to do so? By releasing our old neural pathways to walk on new ones? A decision is nothing more than altered energy. It is this possibility that Invisible Truth puts forth to us.

Some have been courageous enough to name it. Aether. The fifth element. The void. That which cannot be known, only theorized about. The space between what is known and what isn't known. I put to us the fact that scientists have always read science fiction, and then invented that which they learned in fiction. They hypothesis, and given time, they prove what lies in between the known and the not yet known. In that space, can we see what lies there for us?

…Is not known…has not yet been deduced…yet….

Put another way, aether is the medium through which that which is not known becomes known.

I accept that I don't know everything. In fact, I accept that I don't know a lot. The difference that Invisible Truth has made in my life is that I have now chosen to open myself to the realm of all the possibilities within the universe. I have chosen to open my mind, body and soul down to my cellular level, to the concept that I am energy, that I can redirect energy in the way that I choose...that I can, and will, create my own "fate."

I choose greatness.

The Venues of Aether

The senses of the spiritual world are charity, gratitude, peace, humility and faith. Through these we also build the empirical evidence of our world. If we show charity to others, give gratitude for that which we have, are humble in our approach, and have faith (belief) that we are doing the right thing, then we will create peace in our world (our life). All of this is energy. Positive energy. Energy we direct.

Science tells us what the specific energy redirection is through the principles of cause and effect.

Religion, faith, or a belief in a Supreme Being allows us to consciously take the effect of a particular cause, and change it into the start of the next chain of cause and effect that will get us the effect that we desire. We are not victims of the initial effect; we are creators of the next cause (and effect). We have the freewill to choose to create.

One of the basic, routinely accepted premises of science is that for every action there is an equal and opposite reaction. The energy of the love that I give to the world is directly and proportionally reflected back at me in some way, shape or form. Period. End of story. Science states this as law. God says this throughout His teachings.

Religion and science are aiming at the same, identical goal. The laws of the universe are the same as God's laws. It is the contention of Invisible Truth that science deals with cause and effect, and that religion, indeed all spiritual teachings, deal with effect and cause (or effect and cause instead of effect). The universe causes an effect which, instead of letting it affect me, I turn the effect into a new effect because I have the freewill to do so. I redirect the energy. Thus effect...and effect-from-effect.

The will is not free - it is a phenomenon bound by cause and effect - but there is something behind the will which is free.
— Swami Vivekananda

See into the void.

The small portion of our brain that we actually use can ultimately work against us. Through our perception of cause and effect, we create "blocks" in our neural pathways through which the daily masses of information coming at us are filtered. If our filters become clogged, our engines (brains) do not run as efficiently as they could otherwise run.

Through the study, use and application of the Invisible Truth, we are learning to clean out the filters through which the signals of our lives pass, thereby making our conscious and unconscious minds more efficient in creating (manifesting) that which we desire. We are learning to trust ourselves, gaining the freedom to move forward. We are learning to acknowledge our past without dwelling on it in order to clear the space in front of us. With clear space in front of us, we have room to create as we chose.

Analysis is freedom from; Invisible Truth is freedom to.

Aether is the space between what is known and what is unknown. The transmission medium. Open up. See what is moving out there.

When we tap into the universe, and listen very intently (to our gut, instinct, God, Holy Ghost, whatever we wish to call it), we get to choose what cause we are going to be over the effect of the consequence that the universe has brought us.

With clarity, we view the effect of the consequences of the universe's existence. With freewill, we choose to cause the effect we desire, playing by the scientifically universal rules. We redirect positive energy toward our goals. From the facts, we (the creators) pick good energy with which to cause an effect (a goal).

The laws of the universe are set; they give us cause and effect, which, technically, is fate. The laws of God add the factor of US into the equation. Do not accept our fate which was "given" to us by the universe. Choose to redirect our energy. We can; science tells us so. We have the power to redirect a flow of energy. That is a law of nature. We do it every minute of every hour of every day.

With inductive reasoning, inference, a priori, we believe (we have faith) that we can cause the effect we desire with the energy we were given. Scientifically, with deductive logic, a posteriori, we see the empirical proof, the clear factors, the set parameters, the laws of the universe, and we conclude that we can redirect the energy to cause the effect we desire.

Both are expounding cause and effect…and have been since the beginning of time. Both are choosing to control the redirection of energy. One believes it can be done, thus does it. The other sees it can be done, thus believes it. It can be done; we can control our world. The laws of the universe say it is so, empirically and emphatically. Both science and religion tell us so.

We have, within us, the collective consciousness of the history of the universe touching every cell in our being. We are pure energy.

It is time to start listening.

Unveiling the Neural Mystery

Just as your car runs more smoothly and requires less energy to go faster and farther when the wheels are in perfect alignment, you perform better when your thoughts, feelings, emotions, goals, and values are in balance. — Brian Tracy

Isaiah 30:21 Whether you turn to the right or to the left, your ears will hear a voice behind you, saying, "This is the way; walk in it." (NIV)

Defining These Neuropeptides

Let's remove all of the mystery of our impulses jumping through our bodies. We claim that we don't know what they are or how to control them. With knowledge comes understanding. With comprehension comes control. With control comes directed, organized energy heading in the direction of my choice. That is the Invisible Truth.

The following definitions come from **www.Dictionary.com**.

Neuropeptides: Any of various short-chain peptides, as endorphins, that function as neuromodulators in the nervous system and as hormones in the endocrine system.

Neuromodulators: Any of various substances, as certain hormones and amino acids, that influence the function of neurons but do not act as neurotransmitters; something (as a polypeptide) that potentiates or inhibits the transmission of a nerve impulse but is not the actual means of transmission itself.

Receptors: A nerve ending or other structure in the body, such as a photoreceptor, specialized to sense or receive stimuli. Skin receptors respond to stimuli such as touch and pressure and signal the brain by activating portions of the nervous system. Receptors in the nose detect the presence of certain chemicals, leading to the perception of odor.

Short version: Neuropeptides are composed of neural tissue which conducts electrical impulses to convey information and instructions from one part of the body to another. Neuropeptides help convey the instructions to which the body responds accordingly.

Defining neuropeptides was a challenge because they perform several jobs. Definitions sounded contradictory until I looked for the similarities instead of the differences. Here are some of the words I found online, paraphrased:...protein-like molecules used by neurons to communicate with each other...neuronal signaling molecules...a substance, other than a neurotransmitter, released by a neuron and transmitting information to other neurons, altering their activities, by inhibiting, influencing, accelerating, etc....modulating the response to neurotransmitters. There are exceptions to this: there are times when a neuropeptide is either or both a neuromodulator and a neurotransmitter. The more common phrase and use is that of the neuromodulators, thus, that is what we are starting with here.

Okay, the usage question is this: is the neuropeptide the driver (speed influencer) or is it the traffic signal light (directional influencer) or is it high octane (enhancer, booster of power) gasoline (energy) for the car (neuron) that races through the streets and highways of my body (neural pathways) while I am out looking for fun? It is all three of these.

Think of it first as the driver's emotion and we'll add more visualizations, such as the traffic signal light and the high octane gasoline, within the following examples. It is prior to the words (neuromodulators) of the driver (neuromodulator) who is operating the car (neurotransmitter) while talking on the phone (neurotransmitter) and the car itself (neurotransmitter). It is prior to all of that. The first neuropeptide is the emotion.

The reason our driver got into the car was because we felt ecstatically happy. Our brain registered the thought and feeling of "ecstatic" which told our cells, "Gentlemen, start your engines." The happy drivers jumped in their cars, revved them up and took off for the starting line. The traffic signals sent them racing toward the correct receptors within the body. The race cars flew down the streets (neural pathways) to skid into the right garages (receptors).

The receptors are open to their matching neuropeptides only. A happy car cannot park in a sad garage; there's no common ground, no common reality, no matching code, thus it cannot occur. The happy cars will not take the avenues of sadness. The happy and sad avenues (neural pathways) are not interchangeable. Therefore, at the conclusion of the happy car's journey, he will come upon a number of garages (receptors). The only garages accessible to park in are the happy garages. The sad garages have now been locked by us. A lifetime of experience has created the avenues and garages available for the happy and the sad cars to use. Road construction through Invisible Truth is making more avenues accessible which the happy cars can use. We are shutting down the sad highways and locking the sad garages, by our own conscious choice. Open more happy highways.

Let's continue.

Peptide: A chemical compound that is composed of a chain of two or more amino acids and is usually smaller than a protein. The amino acids can be alike or different. Many hormones and antibiotics are peptides.

Polypeptide: A peptide, such as a small protein, containing many molecules of amino acids, typically between ten and one hundred; a molecular chain of amino acids.

Amino acids: Any of a large number of compounds found in living cells that contain carbon, oxygen, hydrogen, and nitrogen, and join together to form proteins. Amino acids contain a basic amino group (NH_2) and an acidic carboxyl group ($COOH$), both attached to the same carbon atom. Since the carboxyl group has a proton available for binding with the electrons of another atom, and the amino group has electrons available for binding with a proton from another atom, the amino acid behaves as an acid and a base simultaneously. Twenty of the naturally occurring amino acids are the building blocks of proteins, which they form by being connected to each other in chains. Eight of those twenty, called essential amino acids, cannot be synthesized in the cells of humans and must be consumed as part of the diet. The remaining twelve are nonessential amino acids.

Less detailed: Basic organic molecules that combine to form proteins. Amino acids are made up of hydrogen, carbon, oxygen, and nitrogen. Some examples of essential amino acids (ones the body cannot make) are lysine, phenylalanine and tryptophan. Some examples of nonessential amino acids (ones the body can make) are arginine, asparagines and aspartic acid. Amino acids are the basic molecular building blocks of proteins.

Neurotransmitters: Any of several chemical substances, as epinephrine or acetylcholine or dopamine, that transmit nerve impulses across a synapse to a postsynaptic element, as another nerve, muscle, or gland.

More detailed: Any one of a number of chemicals that are used to transmit nerve signals across a synapse. They are sprayed from the end of the "upstream" nerve cell and absorbed by receptors in the "downstream" cell. A chemical substance that is produced and secreted by a neuron and then diffuses across a synapse to cause excitation or inhibition of another neuron. Acetylcholine, norepinephrine, dopamine, and serotonin are examples of neurotransmitters. Drugs like Prozac and alcohol affect the emission and reception of neurotransmitters.

Postsynaptic: Being or occurring on the receiving end of a discharge across the synapse; occurring after synapsis.

"…influence the function of neurons." **Neurons**: A specialized, impulse-conducting cell that is the functional unit of the nervous system, consisting of the cell body and its processes, the axon and dendrites.

More detailed: A nerve cell with appendages; Any of the impulse-conducting cells that constitute the brain, spinal column, and nerves, consisting of a nucleated cell body with one or more dendrites and a single axon. Also called nerve cell. A cell of the nervous system. Neurons typically consist of a cell body, which contains a nucleus (the core or center) and receives incoming nerve impulses, and an axon, which carries impulses away from the cell body.

Nucleus: The small, dense center of the atom. The nucleus is composed of protons and neutrons and has a positive electrical charge; the central region of the cell, in which DNA is stored.

"…impulses travel across the synapse…." **Synapse**: Junction between two nerve cells; the place at which a nervous impulse passes from one neuron to another; the junction across which a nerve impulse passes from an axon terminal to a neuron, a muscle cell, or a gland cell.

More detailed: The small junction across which a nerve impulse passes from one nerve cell to another nerve cell, a muscle cell, or a gland cell. The synapse consists of the synaptic terminal, or presynaptic ending, of a sending neuron, a postsynaptic ending of the receiving cell that contains receptor sites, and the space between them (the synaptic cleft). The synaptic terminal contains neurotransmitters and cell organelles including mitochondria. An electrical impulse in the sending neuron triggers the migration of vesicles containing neurotransmitters toward the membrane of the synaptic terminal. The vesicle membrane fuses with the presynaptic membrane, and the neurotransmitters are released into the synaptic cleft and bind to receptors of the connecting cell where they excite or inhibit electrical impulses.

Less detailed: A gap between two nerve cells. Nerve signals are sent across the gap by neurotransmitters.

Back to the Neuropeptides: An endogenous peptide (as an endorphin or an enkephalin) that influences neural activity or functioning.

Endogenous: Resulting from conditions within the organism rather than externally caused.

Enkephalin : Either of two closely related pentapeptides having opiate qualities and occurring especially in the brain and spinal cord; either of two pentapeptides that bind to morphine receptors in the central nervous system and have opioid properties of relatively short duration.

Pentapeptides: A polypeptide composed of five amino acids.

Endorphins: Any of a group of peptides occurring in the brain and other tissues of vertebrates, and resembling opiates, that react with the brain's opiate receptors to raise the pain threshold.

More detailed: Substances produced by the brain that have painkilling and tranquillizing effects on the body. Endorphins are thought to be similar to morphine and are usually released by the brain during times of extreme body stress. The release of endorphins may explain why trauma victims sometimes cannot feel the pain associated with their injuries.

Hormone: A product of living cells that circulates in body fluids (as blood) or sap and produces a specific often stimulatory effect on the activity of cells usually remote from its point of origin; a chemical substance secreted by an endocrine gland or group of endocrine cells that acts to control or regulate specific physiological processes, including growth, metabolism, and reproduction.

More detailed: Specialized cells of the nervous system also produce hormones. The brain itself releases endorphins, hormones that act as natural painkillers. Hormones impact almost every cell and organ of the human body, regulating mood, growth, tissue function, metabolism, and sexual and reproductive function.

Compared to the nervous system, the endocrine system regulates slower processes such as metabolism and cell growth, while the nervous system controls more immediate functions, such as breathing and movement. The action of hormones is a delicate balancing act, which can be affected by stress, infection, or changes in fluids and minerals in the blood. The pituitary hormones are influenced by a variety of factors, including emotions and fluctuations in light and temperature.

When hormone levels become abnormal, disease can result, such as diabetes from insufficient insulin or osteoporosis in women from decreased estrogen. On the other hand, excessive levels of growth hormone may cause uncontrolled development.

Just reading this definition of hormones makes me desire to go eat a healthy dinner to get my minerals balanced.

Putting All of These Definitions Together

The chemical balances of our brains and the neural pathways through which our thought patterns pass are influenced by our neuropeptides. In short, our neuropeptides are the short chains of amino acids, and all that these amino acids are composed of, that hang around the synapses of the brain. These neuropeptides are the traffic signal lights at the millions of junctions in our brains through which neurons (cars) pass. These small protein-like molecules are signals to the neurons (cars) that facilitate communication with each other. These molecules help pass our thoughts and emotions (happiness in our drivers) to every part of our bodies (streets) along the neural pathways (streets). These molecules assist the receptors through which we process life. They are in the words we use to communicate. They are not the cell phones nor the cars; not the bodies nor the vocal cords. They are the voice inflection and laughter, the strength of intention and the positive happiness within the energy.

They are what we put into the message that the neurotransmitter sends.

The neuropeptides are neuromodulators; they affect the neurotransmitters. Modulators. They are the traffic signals, not the cars, nor the drivers, nor the messages from the drivers. They influence the function of neurons (cars), but they do not act as just neurotransmitters (drivers and gasoline in the engine). They (traffic signals) cause the traffic to flow. They boost the gasoline's ability to burn efficiently.

Neuromodulators: Potentiates or inhibits the transmission of a nerve impulse but is not the actual means of transmission itself. For example, we've all felt the rush of excitement. We have an ecstatic sensation (a neuropeptide) when we see a close friend (stimulus). The neuromodulators (peptide enhancing excitement) is the traffic signal light at the intersection, waving our car (neuron) driven by our driver (full of ecstatic sensation) forward (along the neural pathway), and calling out to the driver, "Go, right turn! Go hug your friend!" (neuropeptide).

Neurotransmitter: A chemical substance that transmits nerve impulses across a synapse. That would be the car.

Neural pathways: Those are the streets of the body which we keep clear, clean and free of traffic jams (healthy) with good diet and exercise.

The importance of all of this is the singular fact that we control the neuropeptides (traffic signals).

By cleansing out our bucket we wash clean the streets and allow only the useful neuropeptides on the neural pathways of our lives. We flush out the old, bad neuropeptides (old, bad, habitual thoughts with judgments wrapped in emotions) with our pristine hose. Thus, we effectively flush clean the receptors by never feeding them with any of the old, negative thoughts to which we had gotten them addicted. (Shut down the sad highways and garages.)

We stop feeding the addiction, and the addicted receptors lose their voices. We build new ones by conscious choice. (Open happy highways and garages.)

Some of the daily brain functions the neuropeptides influence include common activities such as: analgesia (absence of pain), behavior, local blood flow, rewards, food intake, learning and memory. These are areas of the body we are retaking control of; being on autopilot here is unwise. Take it off autopilot.

Easy Examples

We can start with these three familiar examples. Again, all of the definitions in this chapter are credited to www.Dictionary.com. I merely spliced them together.

Adrenaline (epinephrine) is the neurotransmitter involved in the flight or fight response when the body "tells us what to do" in a critical situation. Neurotensin is one of the neuropeptides affecting the transmission (enhancing or diminishing the rush of the adrenaline or, conversely, the dopamine) of the neurotransmitter which is "telling you what to do." We each already know our personal, favorite causes of adrenaline!

Substance P is an important neuropeptide related to the transmission of pain information into the central nervous system. It has been associated with the regulation of a list of functions including mood disorders, anxiety, stress, pain and inflammation. Substance P and other sensory neuropeptides can be released from the peripheral terminals of sensory nerve fibers in the skin, muscle and joints. Capsaicin (the heat in hot peppers) affects our Substance P's assistance to the body, so researching that may be informative to us. Currently, Substance P is being studied in relation to diabetes, ulcer healing and the stimulation of cell growth. Note that capsaicin, hot peppers, salsa and hot sauce are the most useful items we can add to our diet; they are the one means of increasing our metabolism that is both natural and easy. We can take control of burning the engine of our body more efficiently.

Serotonin is a neurotransmitter that is involved in sleep, depression, memory and other neurological processes. Serotonin is the neurotransmitter and substance P is one of the neuropeptides influencing its behavior. The result of their balancing act is that we sleep well. Adding some healthy natural carbohydrates into our meals will assist with our serotonin balance.

The third one is GABA. GABA is an important neurotransmitter in the central nervous system, regulating both excitability and muscle tone. Neuropeptide Y is a 36-amino acid peptide neurotransmitter found in the brain and autonomic nervous system. It functions in relation to quite a few physiologic processes within the brain, including the regulation of energy balance, memory, learning, and other functions. The main effect is the increase of food intake and the decrease of exercise. GABA is influenced by Neuropeptide Y, however in this instance Neuropeptide Y functions also as a neurotransmitter.

Some neuropeptides function as neurotransmitters in addition to as neuromodulators. Substance P actually does that, however, for the depth of understanding here, it is sufficient to recognize that neuropeptides are first called neuromodulators (influencers) and then (sometimes) neurotransmitters when they achieve larger results within the body systems. That line of delineation (level of responsibility and performance) is easily crossed by the neuropeptides.

As a side note here, reading these definitions may have incited us to take responsibility for our physical mental health. We can attain the amino acids our body requires through protein sources (meat, eggs, seafood) or in meals of whole grains with beans, peas, soy, nuts and seeds.

What This All Means

Inciting ourselves to emotional health begins with the decision. Decide to embrace the Invisible Truth. Start by switching our murky hose to our pristine hose. See the muddy water flow out of our bucket which is becoming filled to overflowing with pristine water.

Whenever an old, addictive behavior raises its voice, whether from the exterior stimuli, the resultant emotion, the neuropeptide or the receptor, see it for what it is and choose a positive reaction instead.

It is our choice.

As we have said before, our original experiences give us a basis of belief. These beliefs are physically formed in our brains. In other words, our transmitters become programmed to receive information from outside of ourselves in a certain prescribed method. Hence, we become "addicted" to the way we think. When a signal comes into our brain, it is automatically filtered through a series of transmitters that send the signal through a prearranged pathway in order to process the data.

We can change the filter. Choose new, healthy and happy addictions.

An Analogy

I will use an analogy for one of the types of neural pathways that we can see working in our lives. We are in our car on the streets of our brain, sitting in "park," waiting for the signal to "go." We know what our desired destination is and have programmed it into our GPS system. However, our GPS system is based on maps that are 20, 30, 40 or more years old. Our system was built before there were even highways. Not only that, but our GPS system has recorded each accident which has occurred in the past years (the span of our life) and has never bothered to clear them from its databank.

A signal comes to us (a stimulus from outside of ourselves) to go. We accelerate and go one block where our GPS tells us to turn left. We go one more block and it tells us to turn right. This goes on through thousands, if not millions, of turns all based on mostly accurate data and some on out-of-date and inaccurate information...and man, were we speeding. We went through thousands, if not millions, of directional changes in less time than it takes us to blink our eyes. We could see the highway we wished to be on, but kept getting further and further from it due to the directions our out-of-date GPS was giving us.

The worst case scenario is that we would never get to where we desired to be. The best case is that we would get there, but after the "never ending detour."

The question is this: what if our GPS system was up-to-date? We only get one GPS system when we are born. If we don't keep our machine up-to-date with current, constantly changing conditions, we either never get to where we desire, or it is going to take us much longer than we wished.

It would be a lot easier to keep our GPS system programmed with current information.

Sometimes we are just out cruising. We are driving through our lives with no real destination in mind. Our GPS is telling us where to go, even though we don't have a desired destination. We are becoming stressed with traffic, and decide that the way to deal with that is stopping at every fast food joint along the way...or having another drink...or smoking another cigarette...or yelling at our kids and spouse. (Sound like it might be hitting a little too close to home?)

Keep studying. The study of Invisible Truth is a method through which we reprogram our GPS with accurate and current information. They also help us create our desired destination.

Now, there is no more mystery inside of our physical body. Our body belongs to us. That was the whole purpose of the chapter, to remove the mystery. Take control. Reprogram our neural pathways by our own conscious choice.

Many persons have a wrong idea of what constitutes true happiness. It is not attained through self-gratification but through fidelity to a worthy purpose. — Helen Keller

It is our life. It is our peace of mind. It is all up to us.

Part Four

Even More Stuff

About the Author

Christina Wollebek-Smith's creation originated around the popularity and reemergence of the Laws of Attraction. She felt there was something missing. The questions were formed amongst her associates. Are the Laws of Attraction real? Are there duplicatable scientific studies available regarding this concept? If so, how do the Laws of Attraction relate to faith based philosophies, and how is that relationship backed up scripturally?

Though she directed the efforts in Invisible Truth, she is the first to tell us that these ideas and concepts are not new. They have been around since the beginning of time. Having always treaded an enthralling and adventurous path through her life, Christina knew the importance of answering these pertinent questions. She learned and experienced a vast variety of teachings and trainings through the years and knew that there was a way to bring everything together that would inspire people, and create lasting results.

Christina was born in Oslo, Norway. Her family immigrated to the United States when she was three. They settled in the Pacific Northwest. Now, she is the proud mother of two amazing children who reside in the same area.

Personal Stories

For 38 years I have had a private issue for which I have gone to counseling and sought solace through self-help books, all to no avail. After studying *Invisible Truth* I have been able to overcome the problems of the past. After six months I have found myself being able to continue living without any reoccurrences and with more peace and happiness. Thank you!
L.B., Indiana

It took me three years to grow my business to the level it was at. After going through the *Invisible Truth*, I increased my business 50% within 30 days.
W.E.M., Sacramento, Ca.

As a certified coach, I've spent over $20,000 on self-help training and materials but nothing can compare to the divine power of this program. After applying the materials from the course, *Invisible Truth*, positive changes have been continually happening in my life at record speeds!
J. G., Sacramento, Ca.

Invisible Truth has been life altering for me. It taught me how to align with and tap into the Divine Power, which I attribute to saving a failing relationship and business. Both have now expanded exponentially by over 400%.
Donna M. Laurel, Indiana

I have a library that consists of thousands of dollars worth of self-improvement courses. I have spent years searching for the program that has long-term results. *Invisible Truth* is the one I choose and recommend. I have not been this happy this consistently for over 20 years. Every human being should have the power of Invisible Truth.

W. D., Michigan

I have spent over $5,000 in different programs over the last several years. After listening to the CDs, I would give them all up to have the *Invisible Truth* course. This is the most understandable and usable course I have ever heard. It is like no other. You can feel the power coming through the stereo speakers.

S. S., Newport News, Va.

I had approximately 10 days to come up with $30,000. My resources were exhausted. The money showed up unexpectedly from an individual who I have never met personally. That is manifestation! Thank you, *Invisible Truth*!

C. W., Seattle, Wa.

As a supplier to numerous Networking companies and their distributors, I highly recommend *Invisible Truth*. This key tool supports personal and group growth for any company. This is on the "A" list for business success, producing excellent results.

Nathan Cox, Sound Concepts

Notes

Law and Principle # 1 Living in the Now

1 C.G. Jung and Wolfgang Pauli, *The Interpretation of Nature and Psyche* (New York: Pantheon Books, 1955).

Cosmic Consciousness

1 **www.Dictionary.com** (Accessed March 1, 2011).

2 **www.StudyOfOahspe.com,** P. 1 (Accessed March 1, 2011).

The laws and principles that govern our lives all lead to one omnipotent, universal realization:

Love is God.

Made in the USA
Columbia, SC
28 August 2017